FIT ASIAN

Peter Slater

Bloke

Exercise to live. Never live
to exercise.
Jack LaLanne

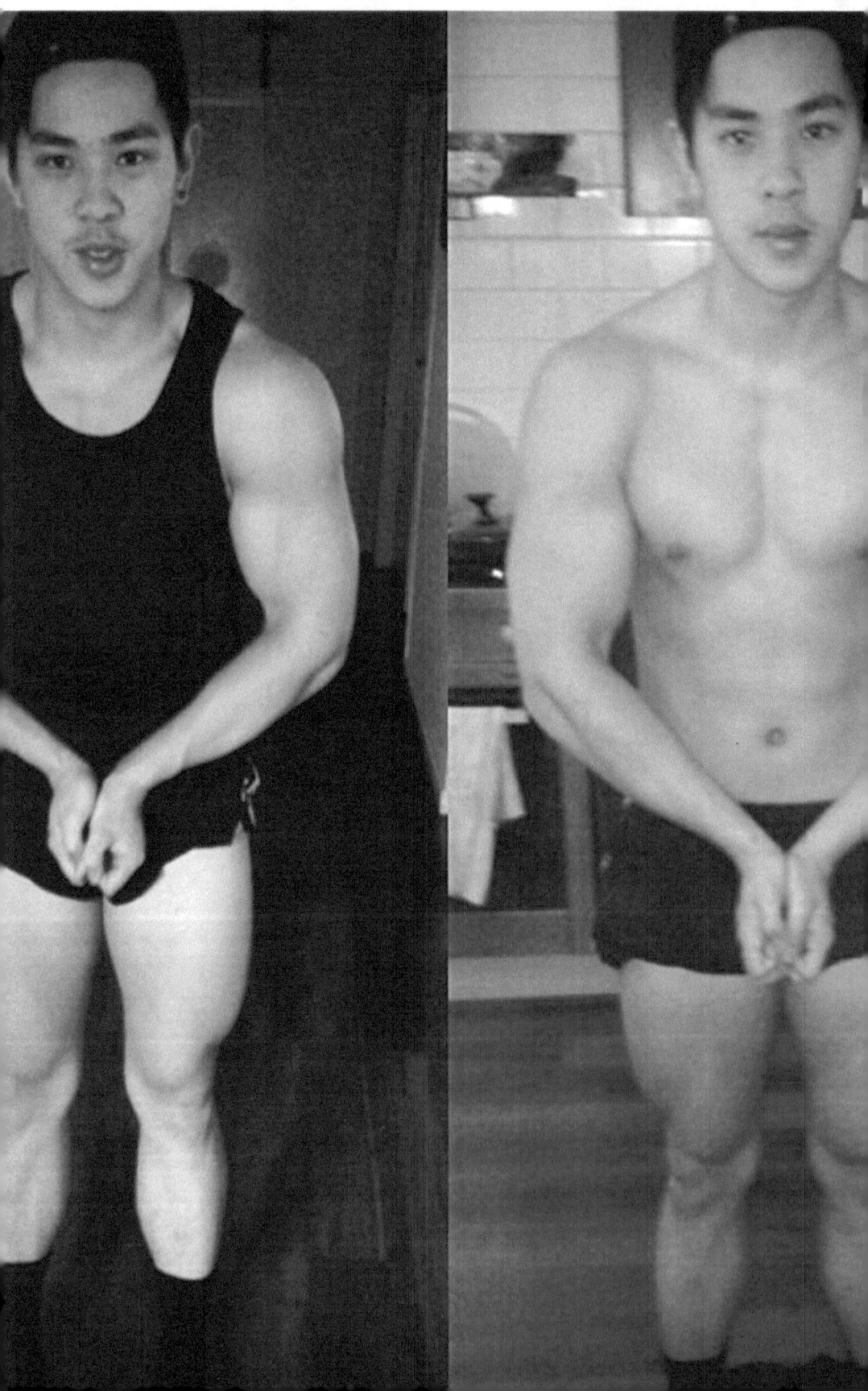

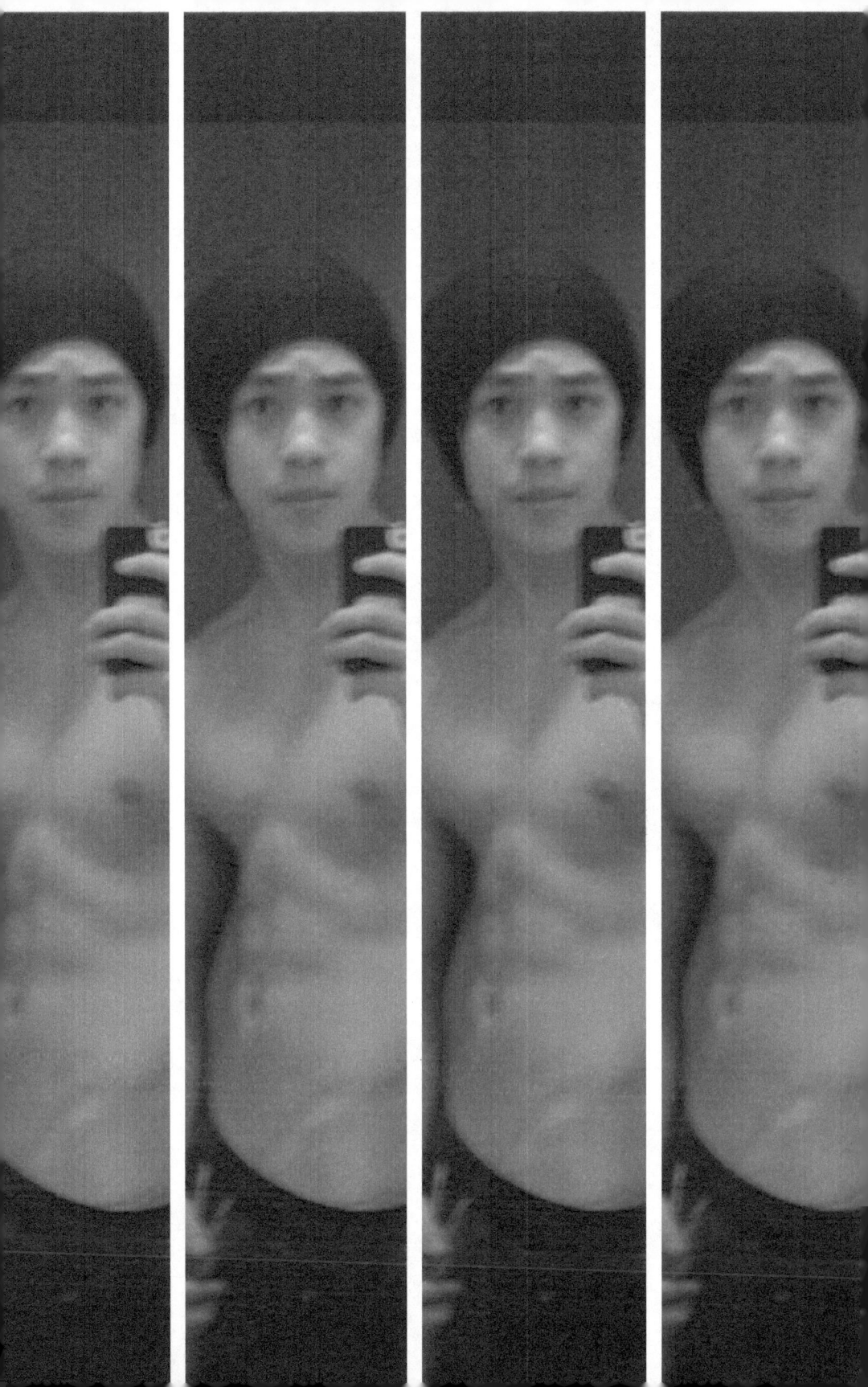

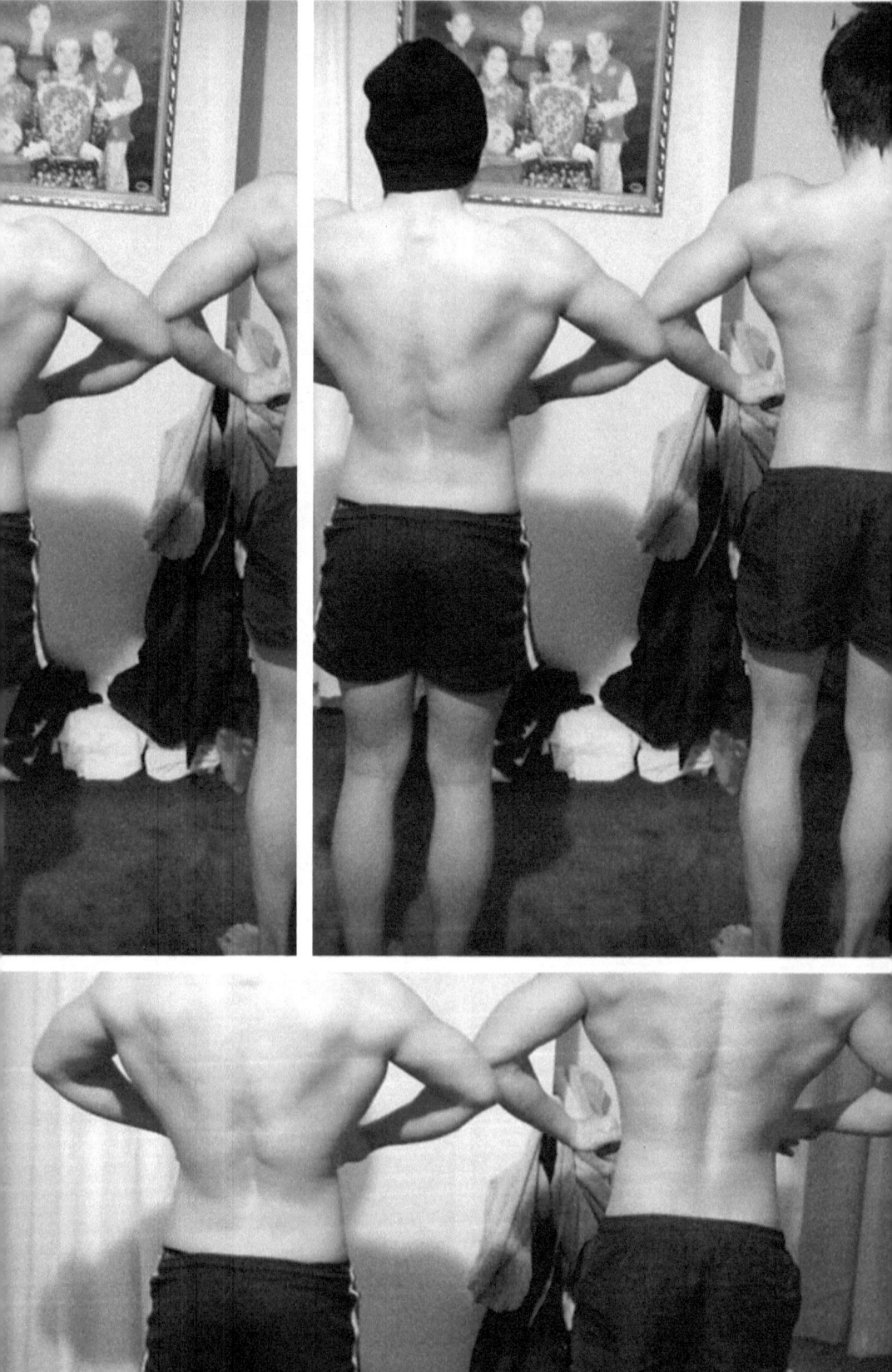

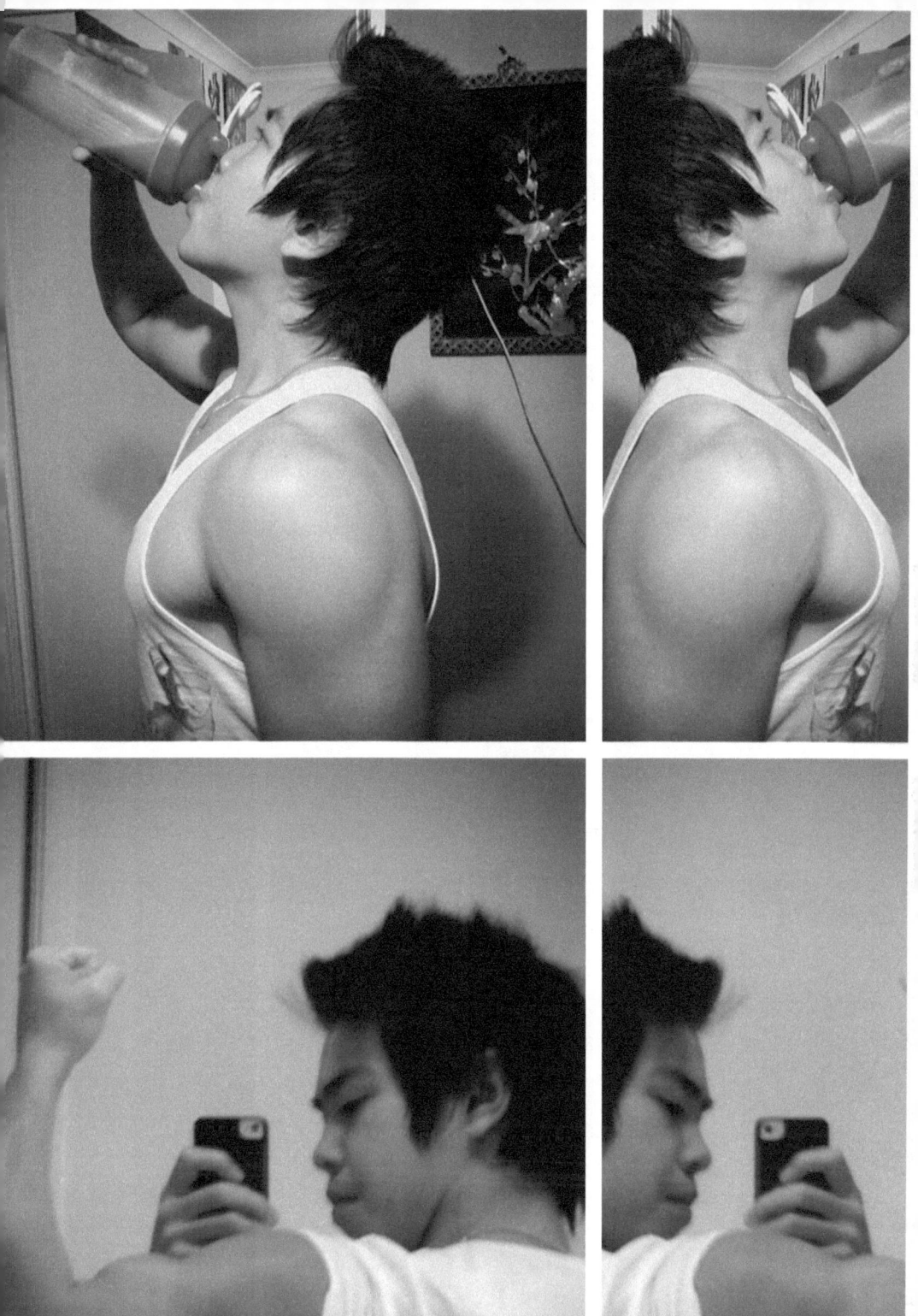

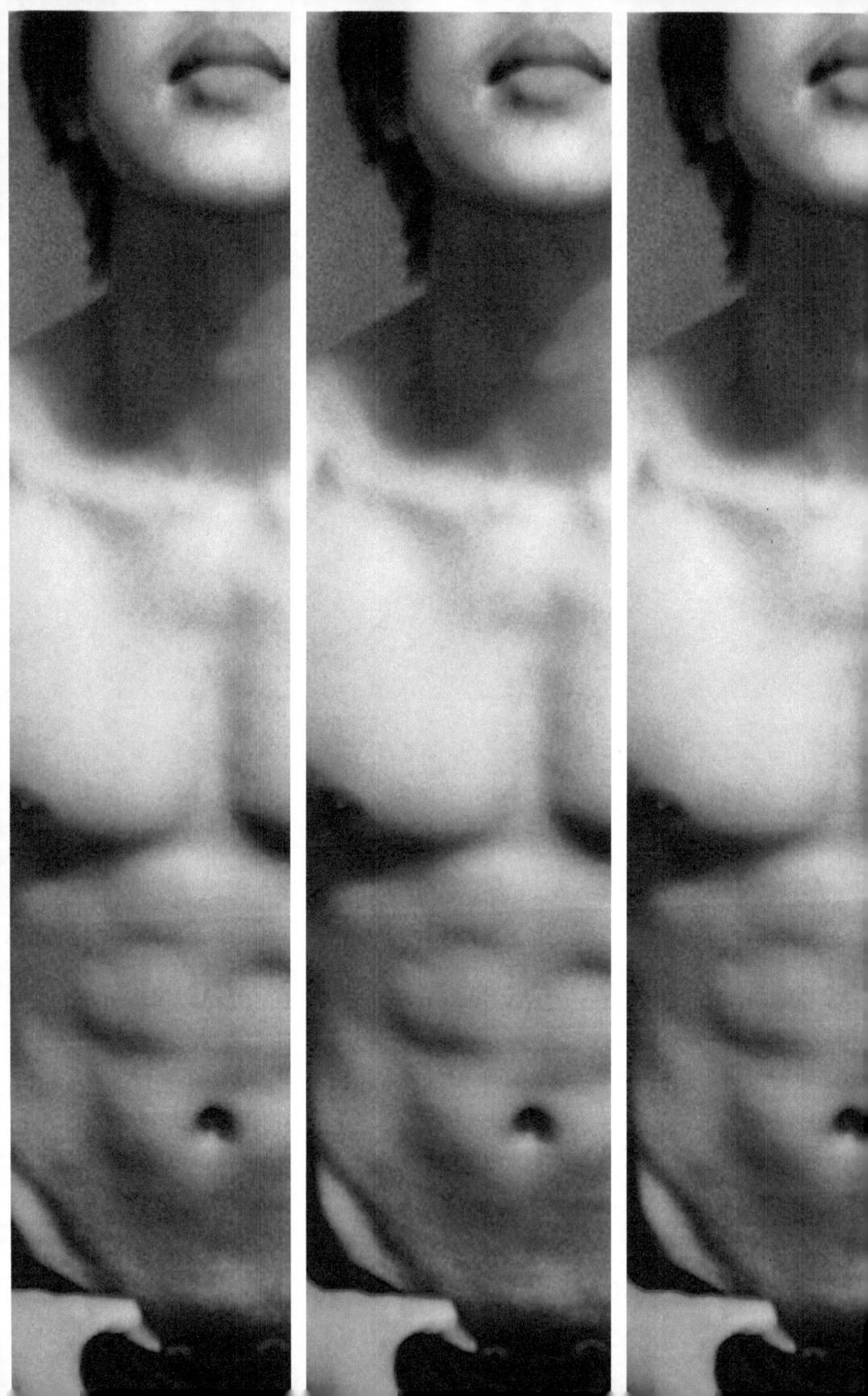

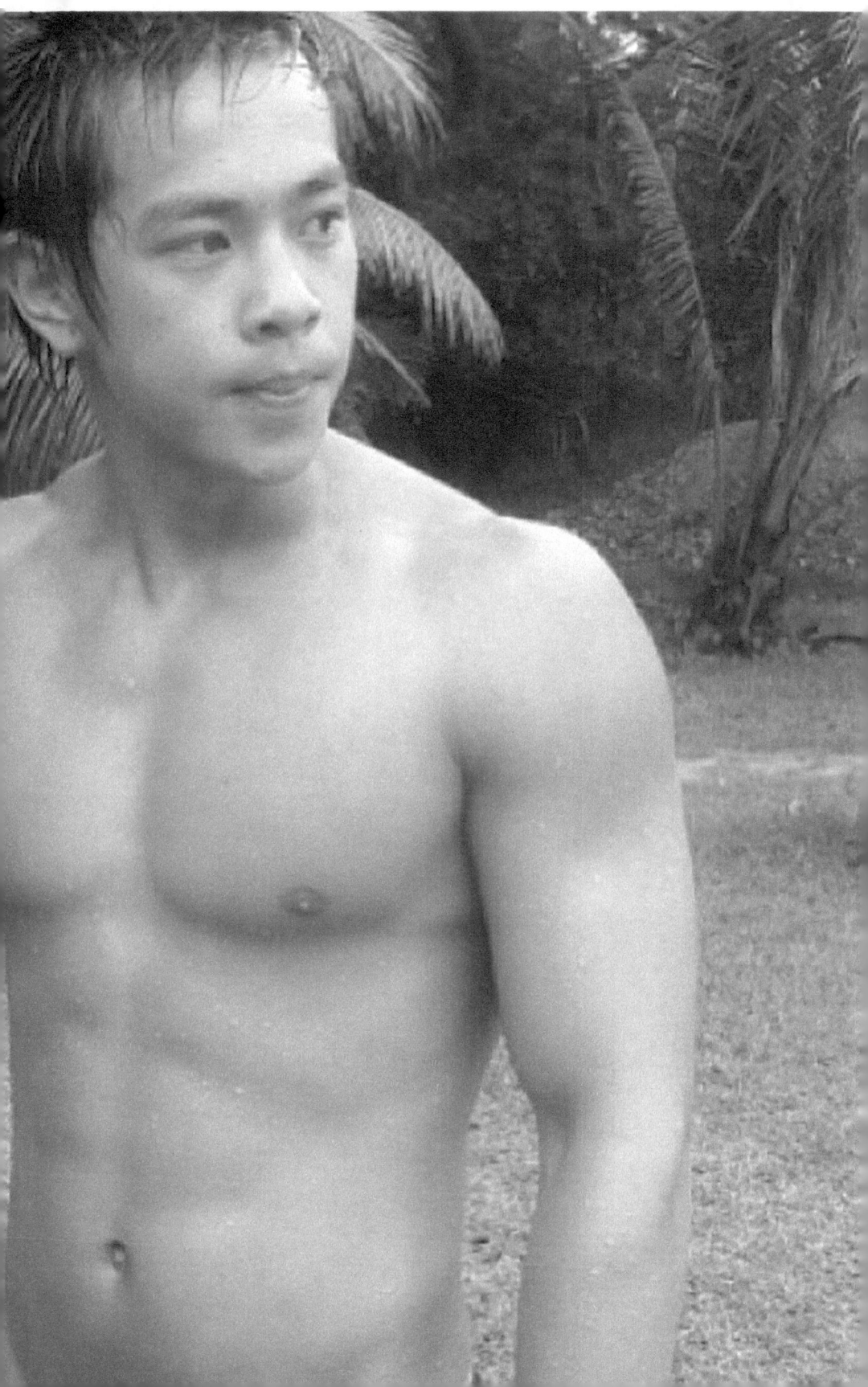

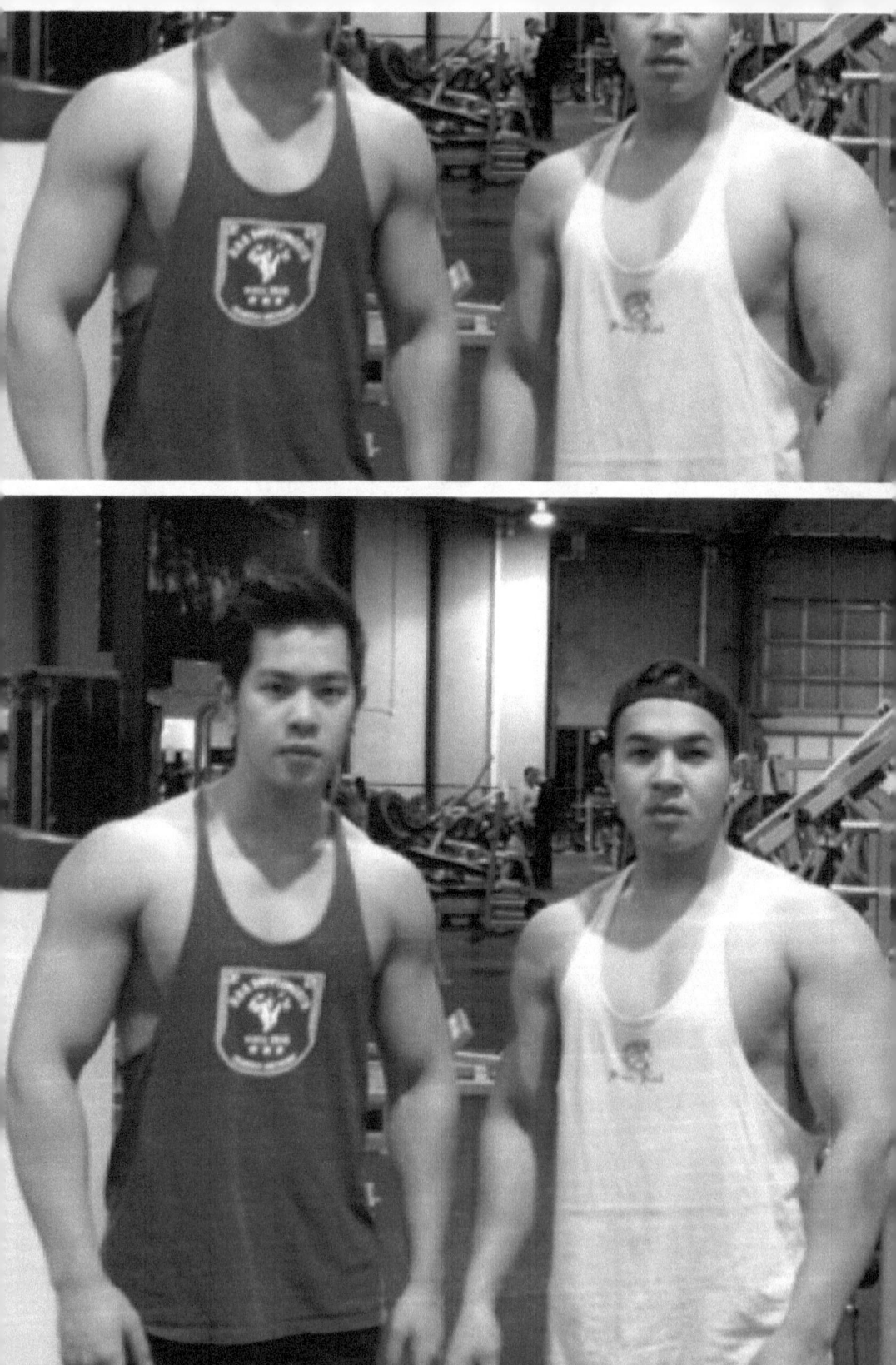

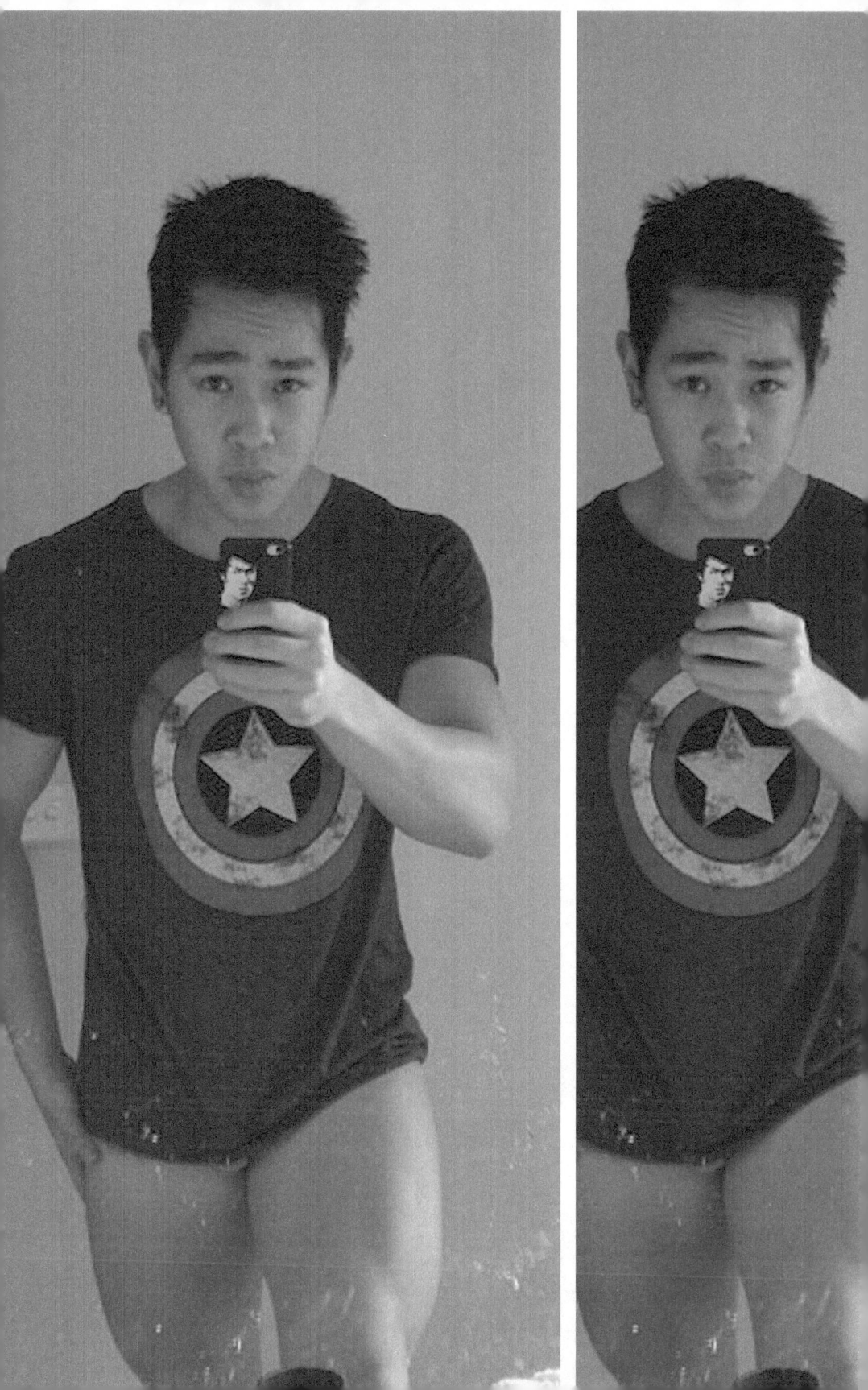

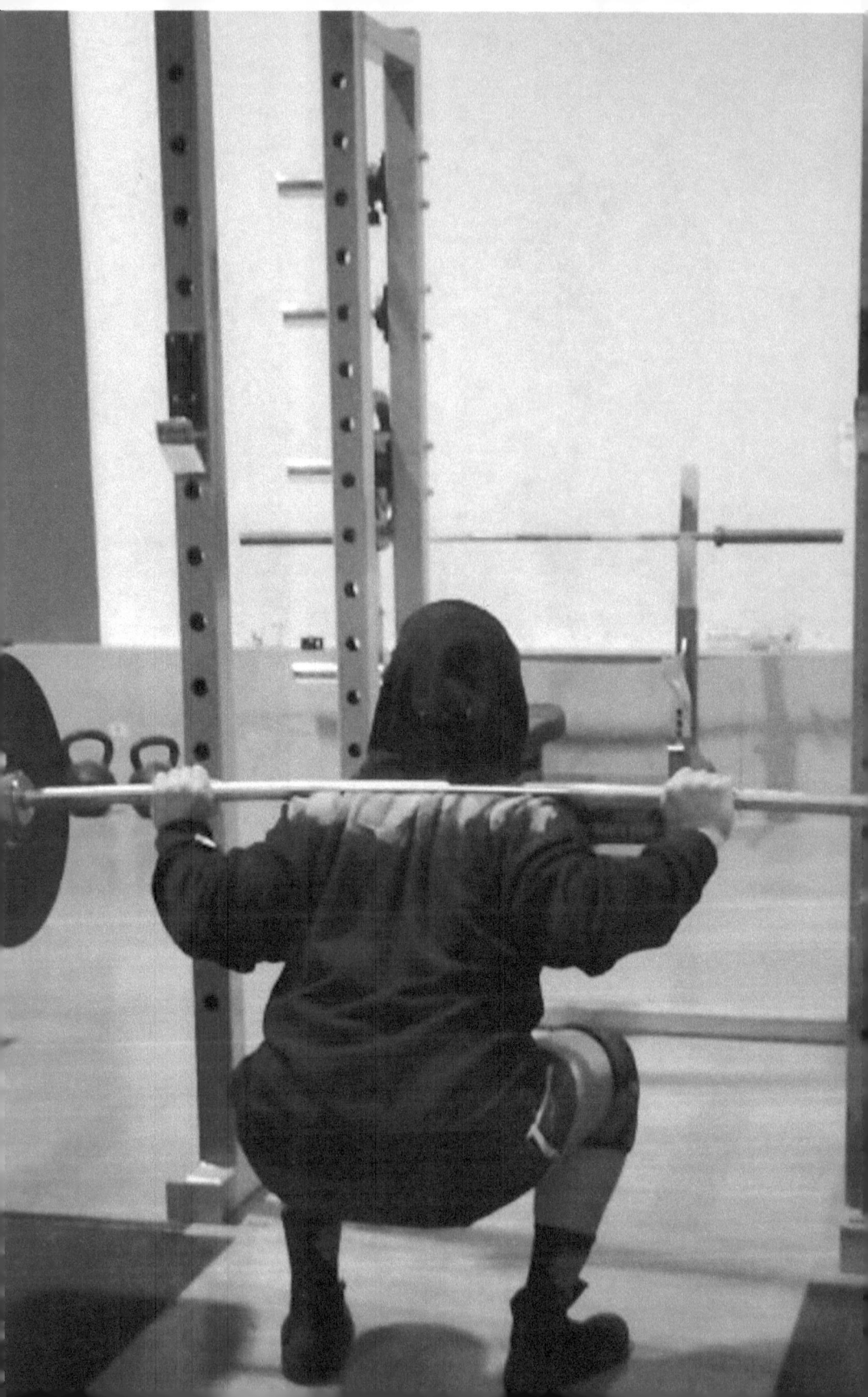

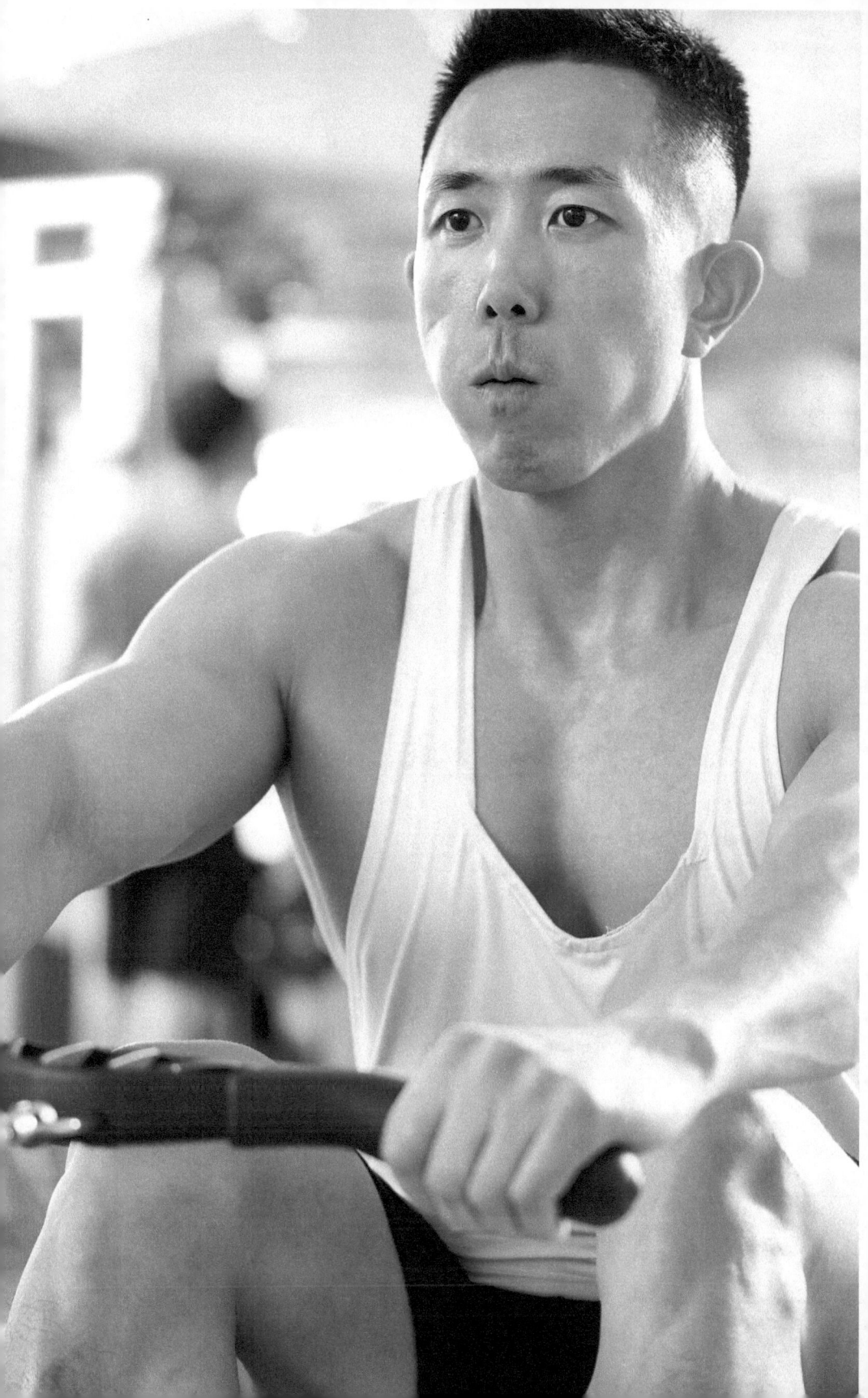

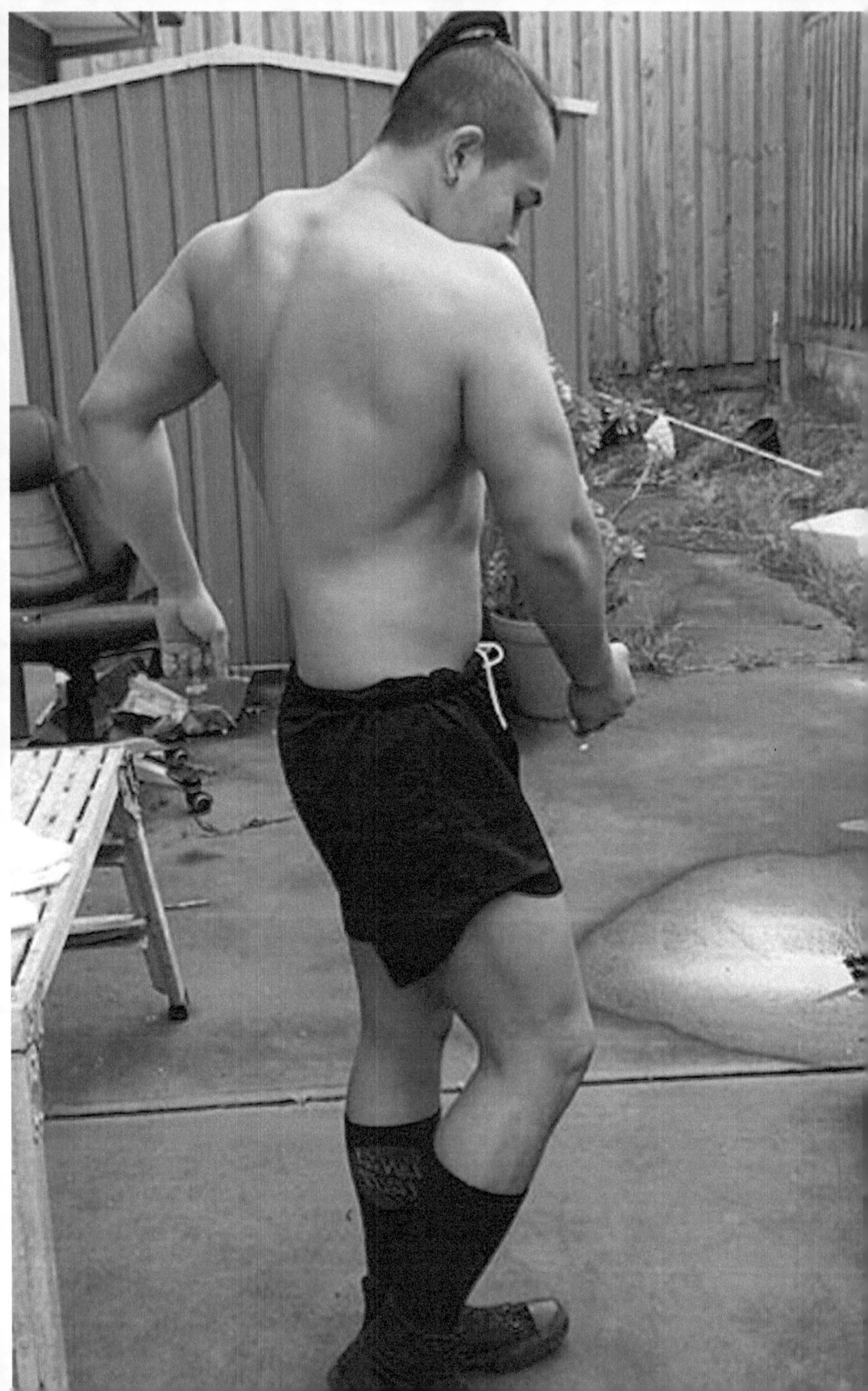

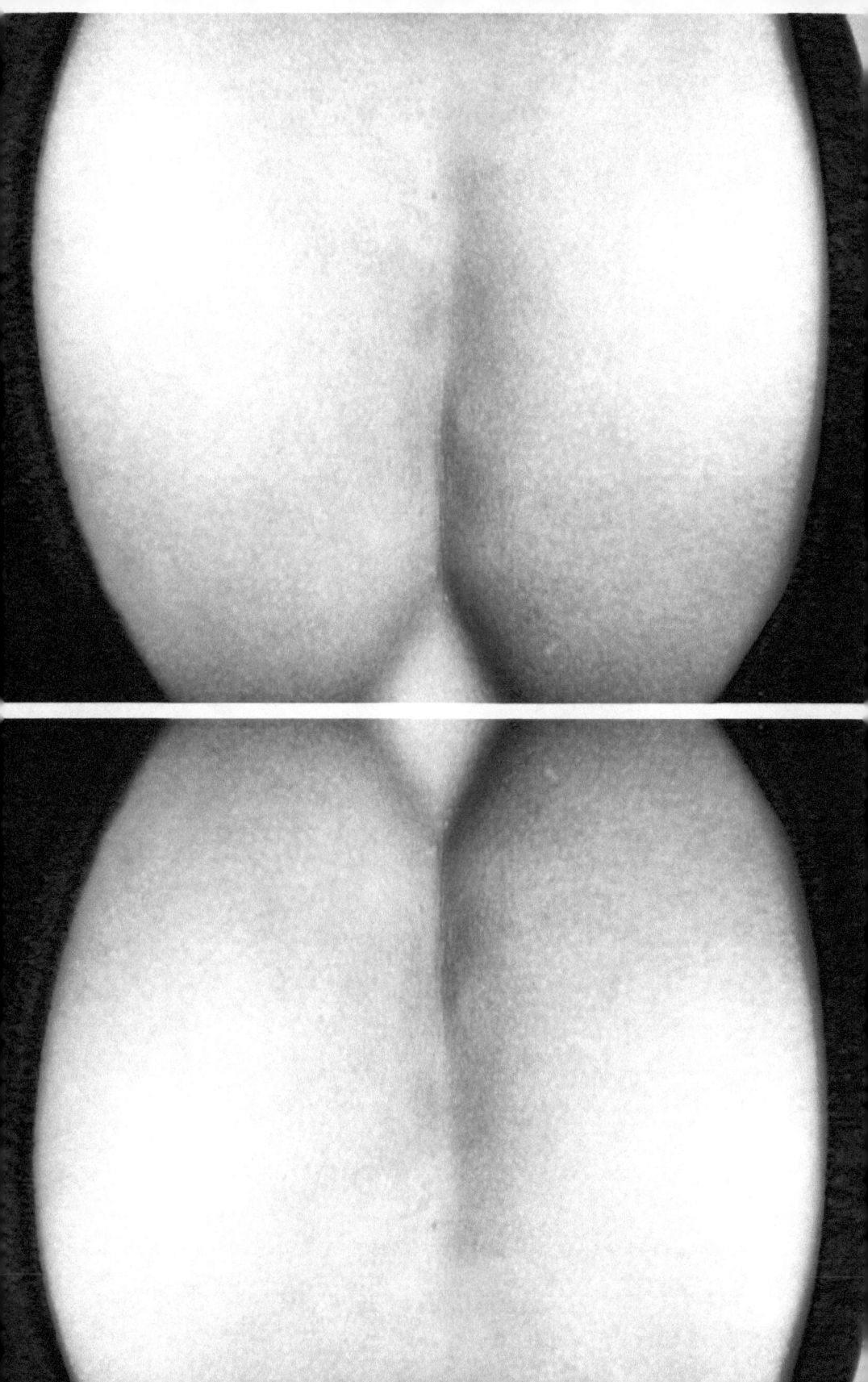

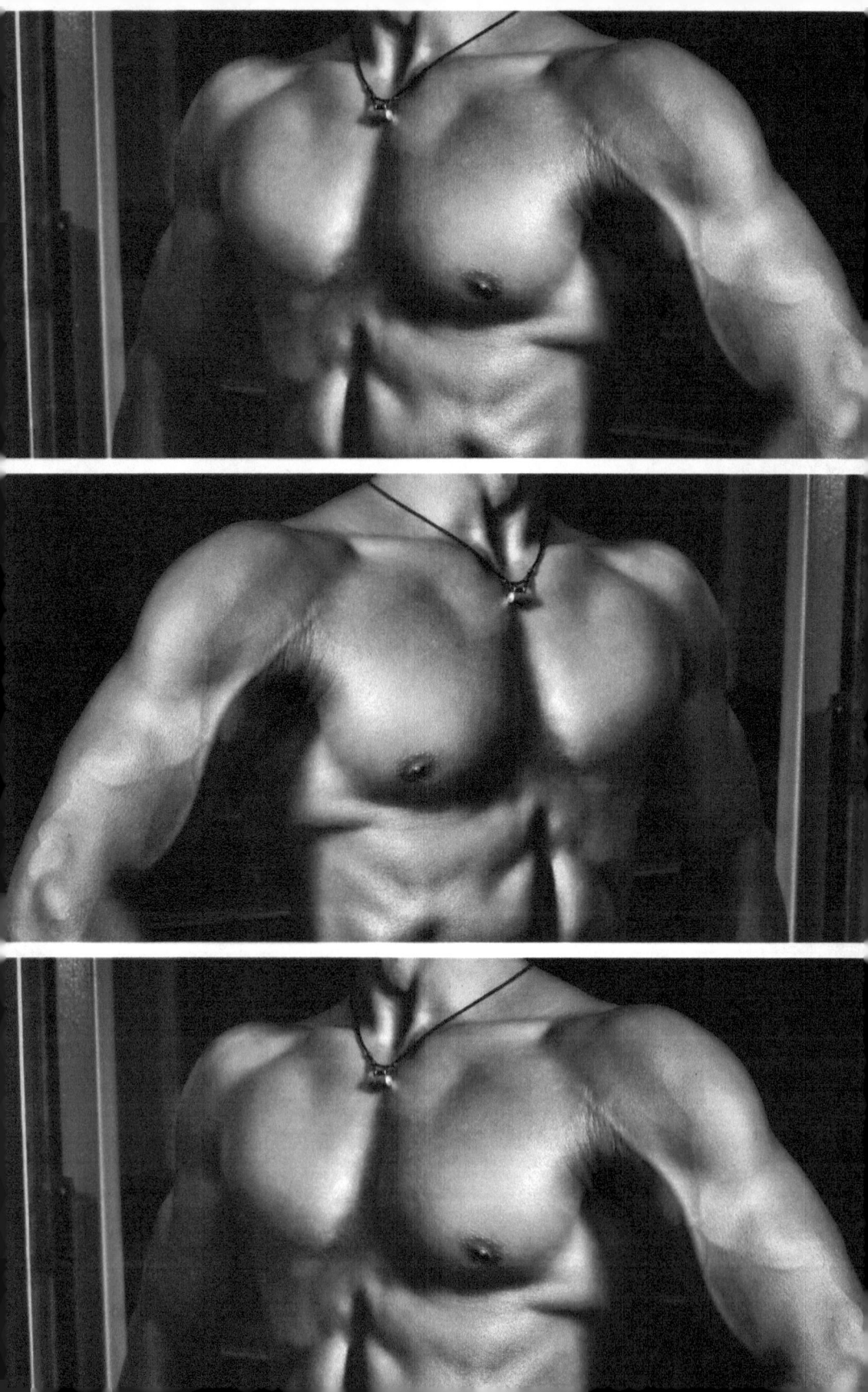

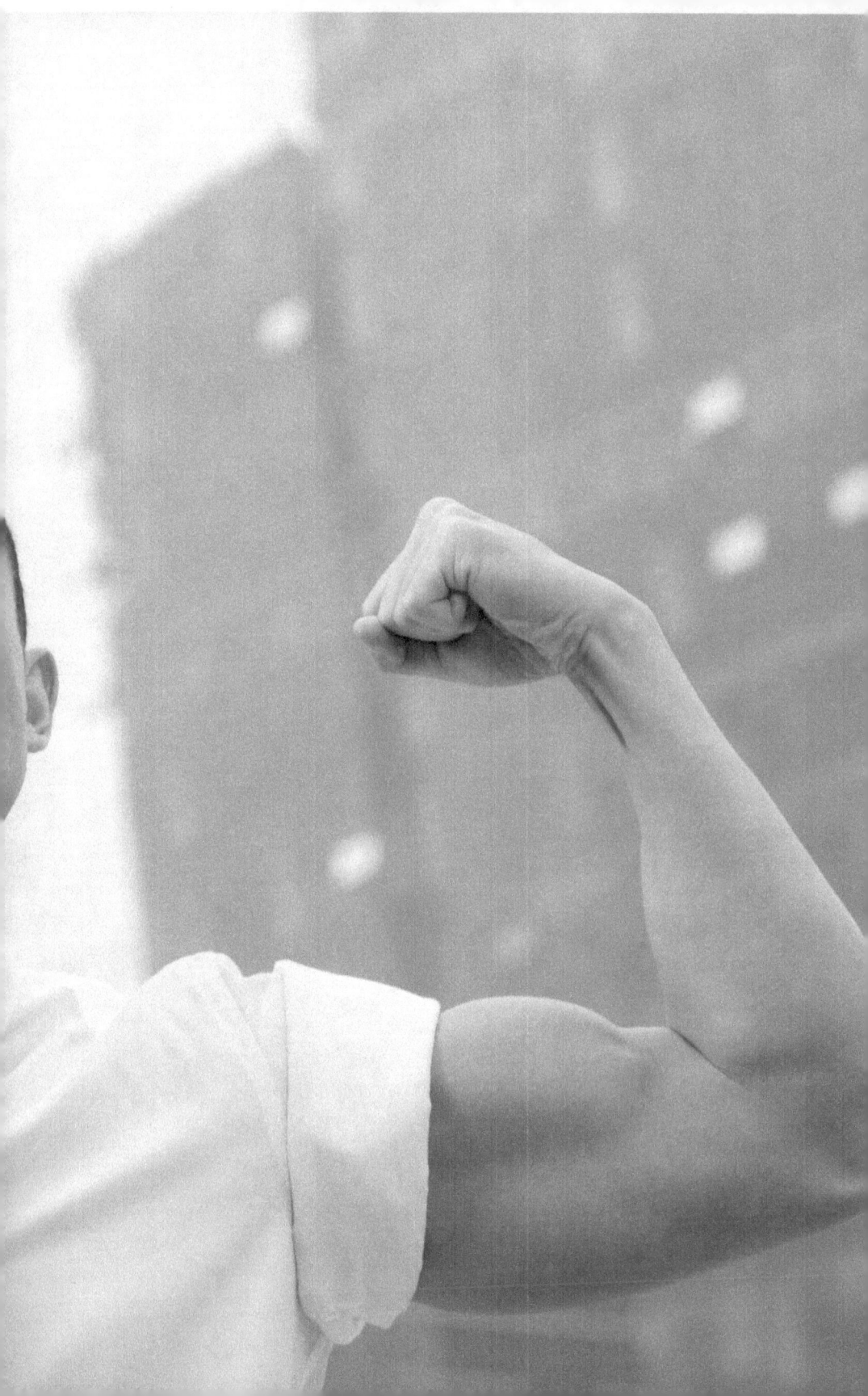

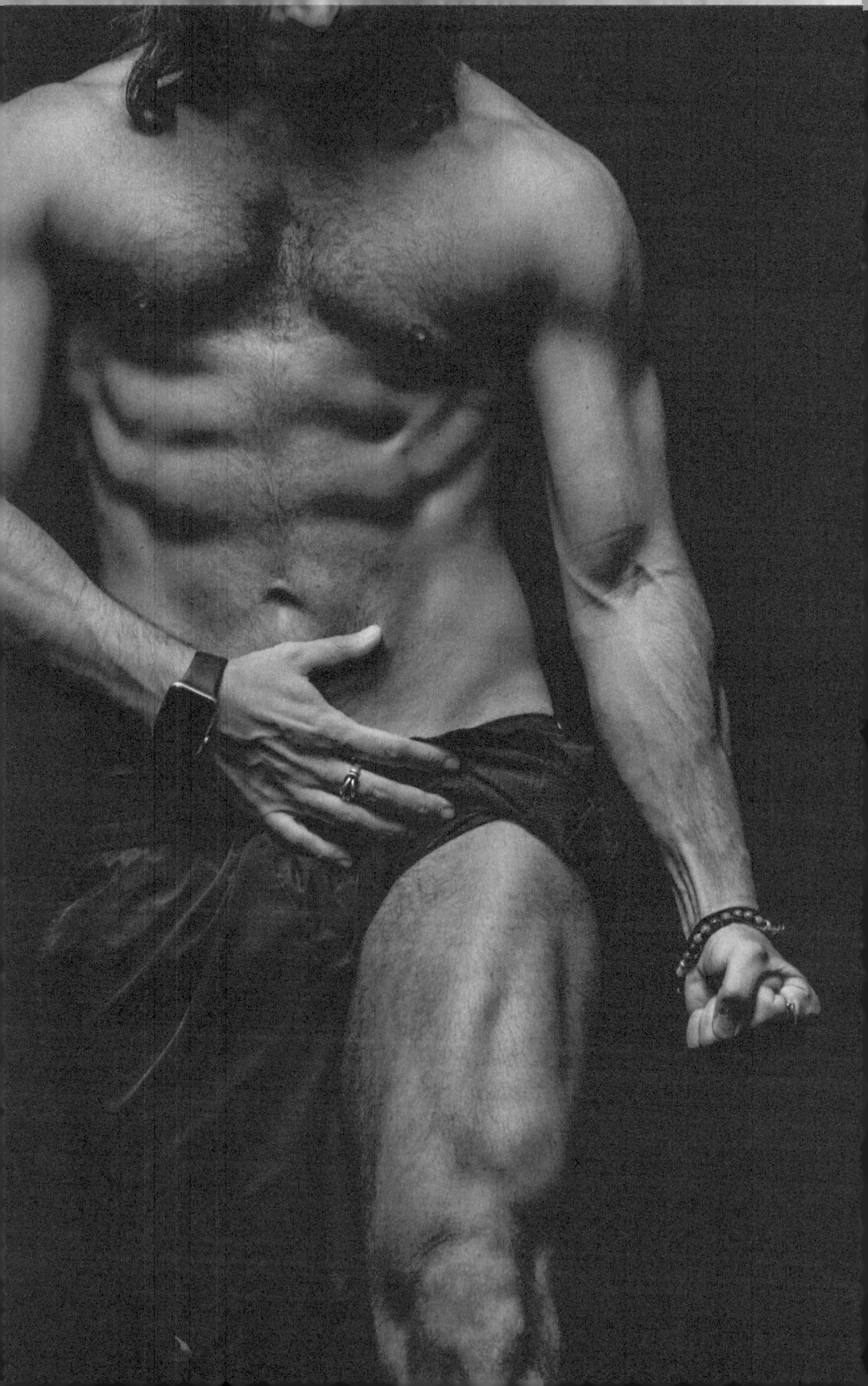

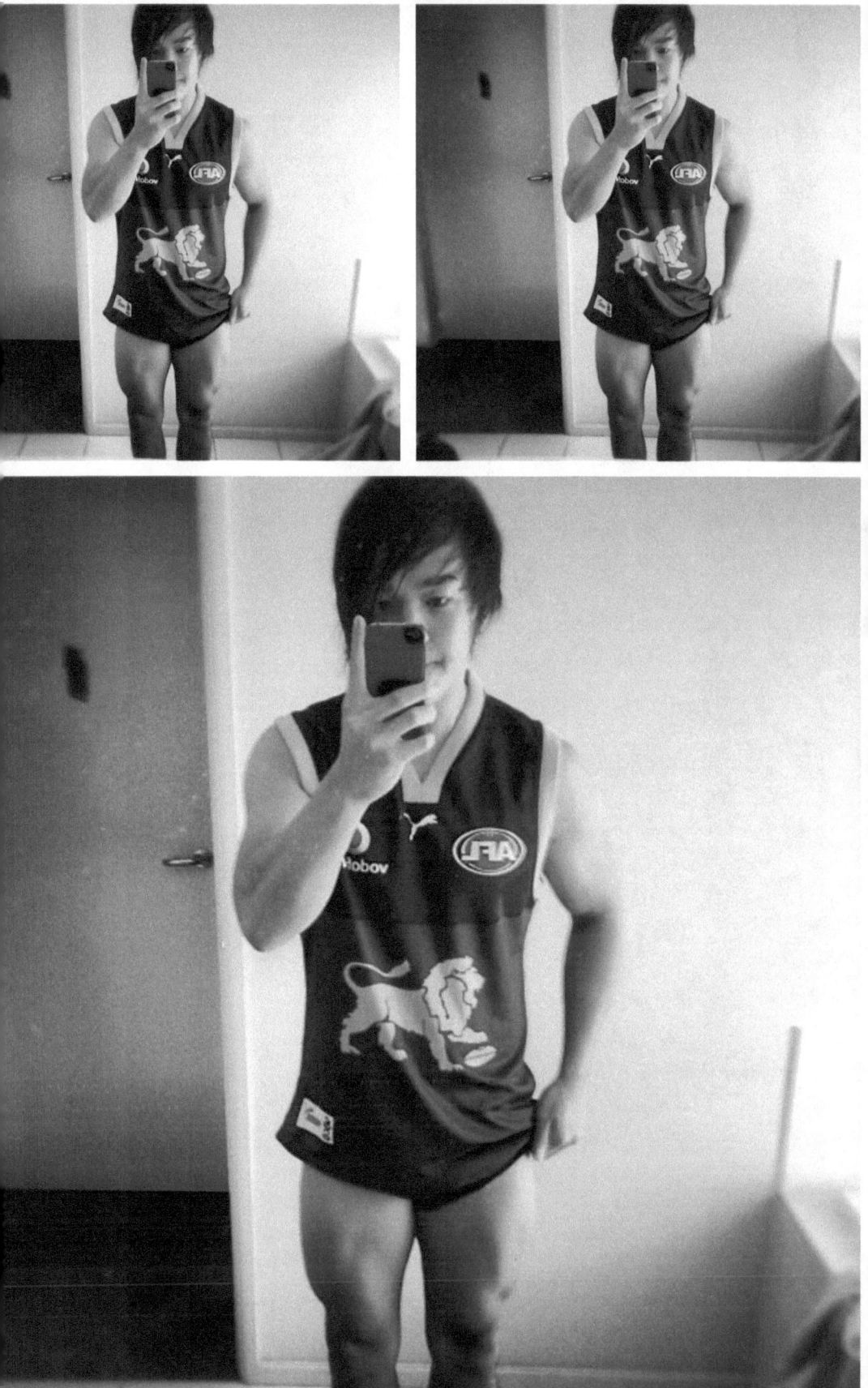

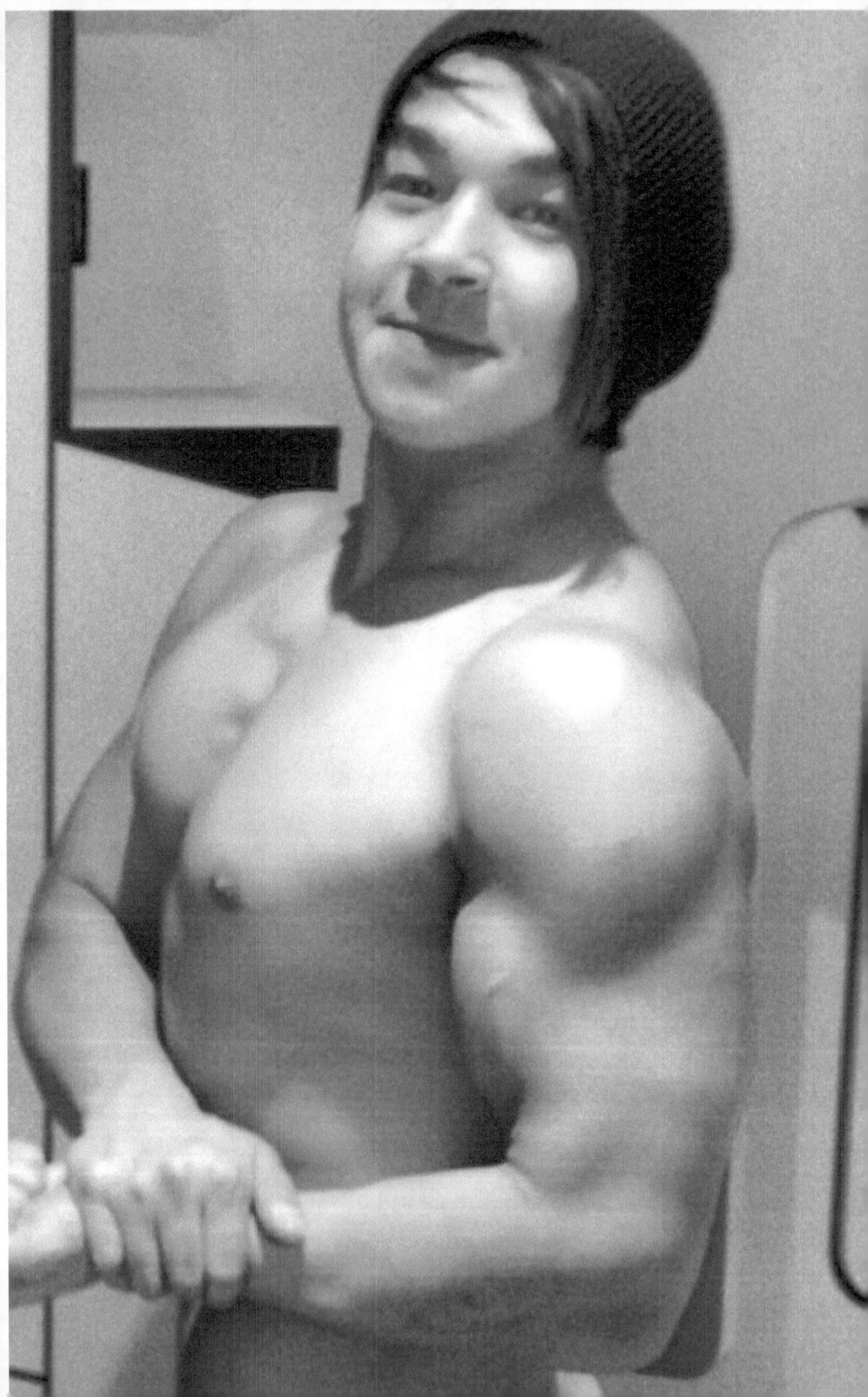

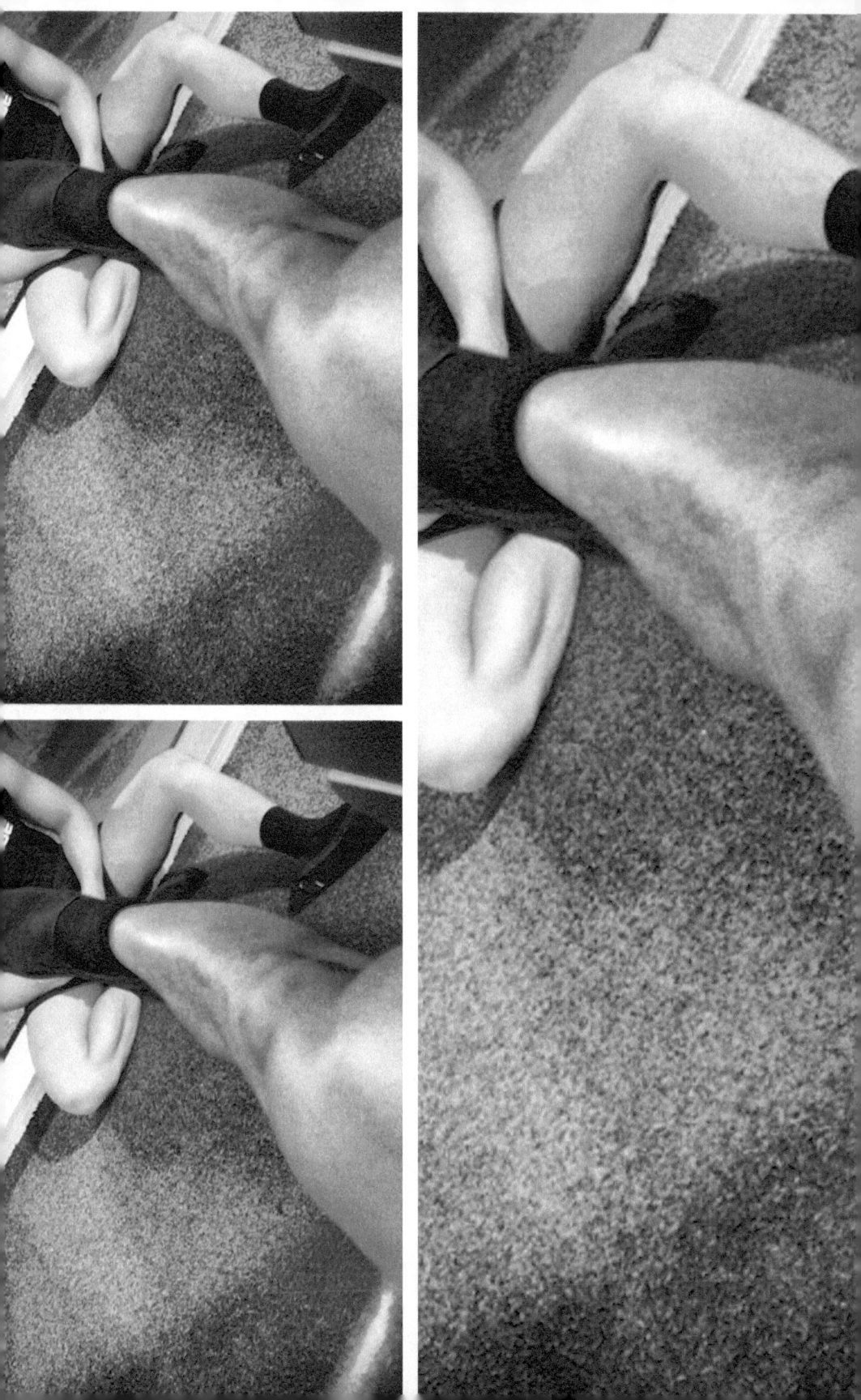

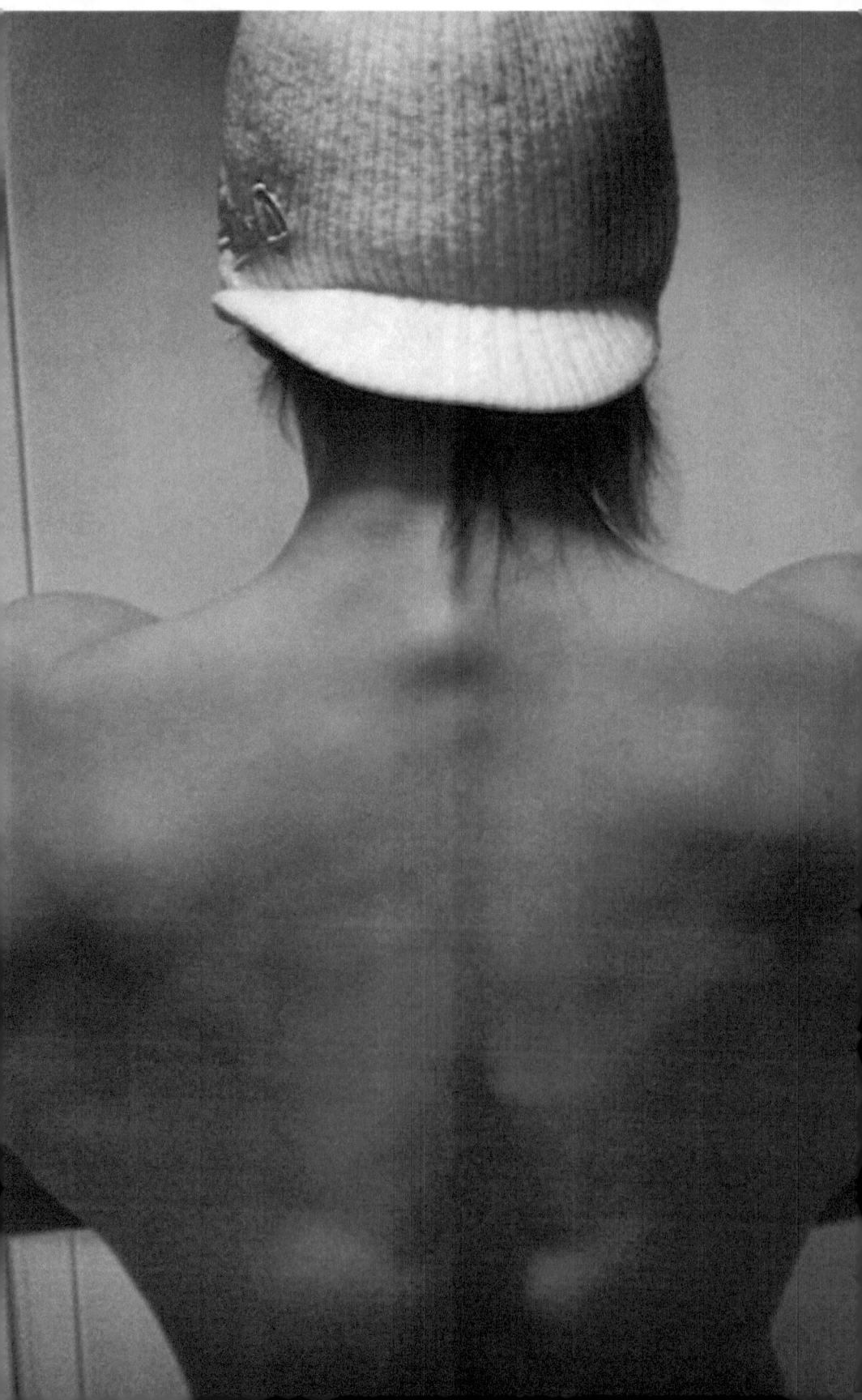

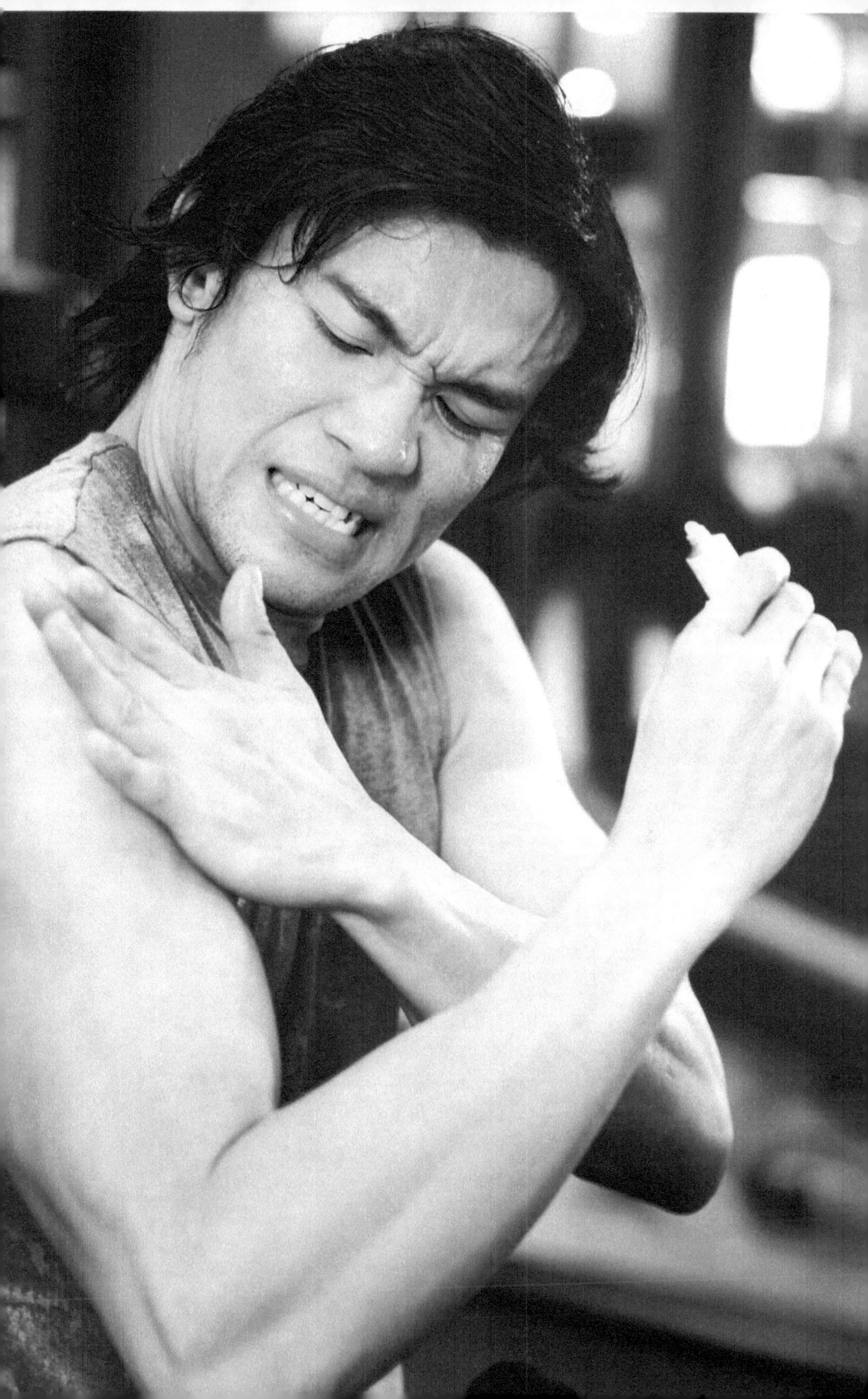

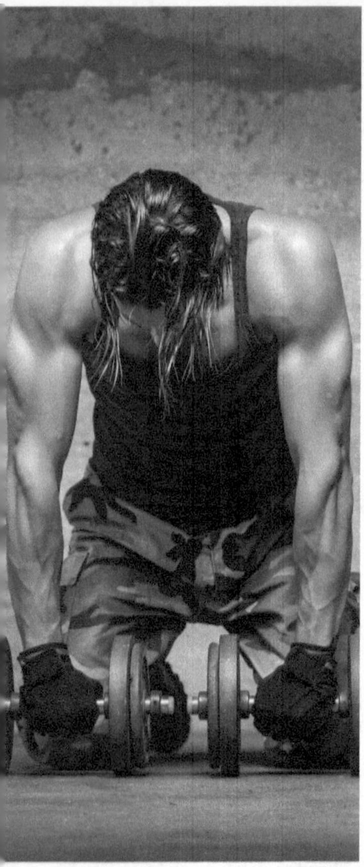

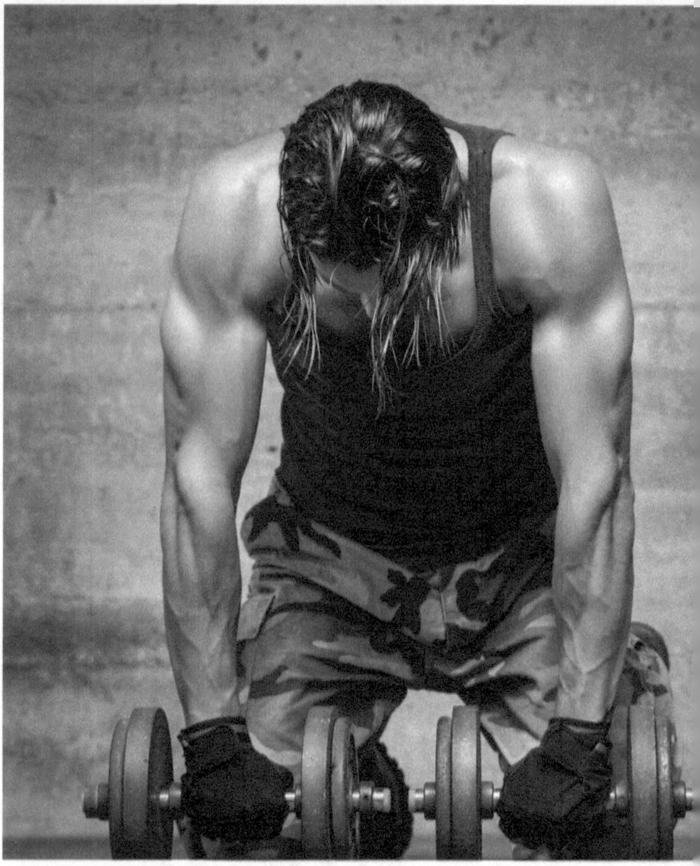

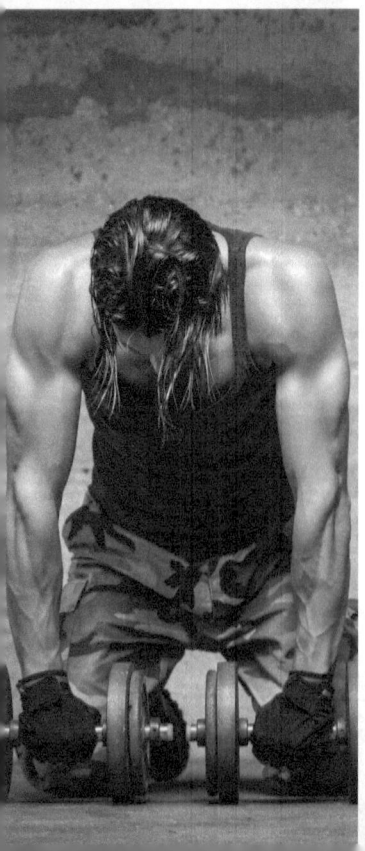
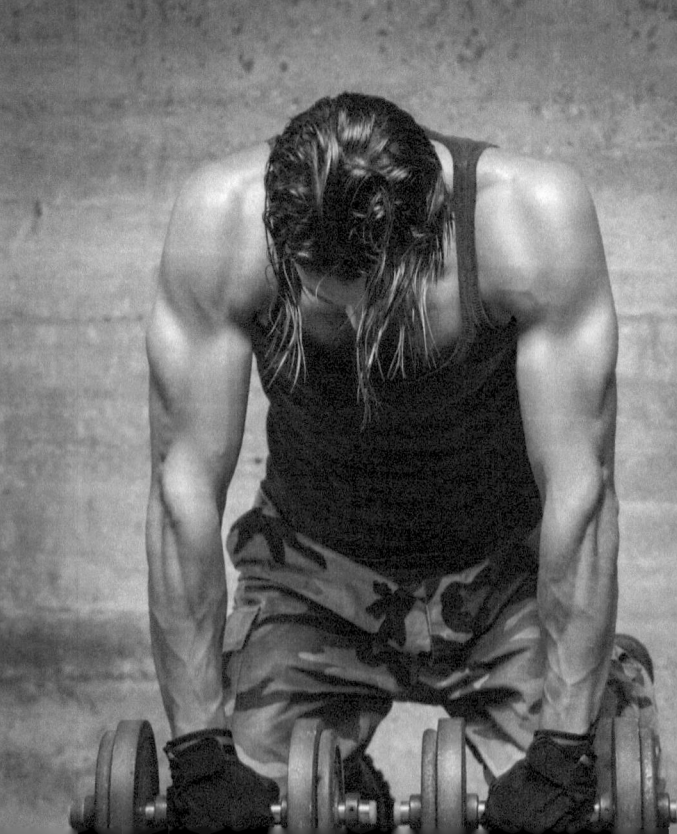

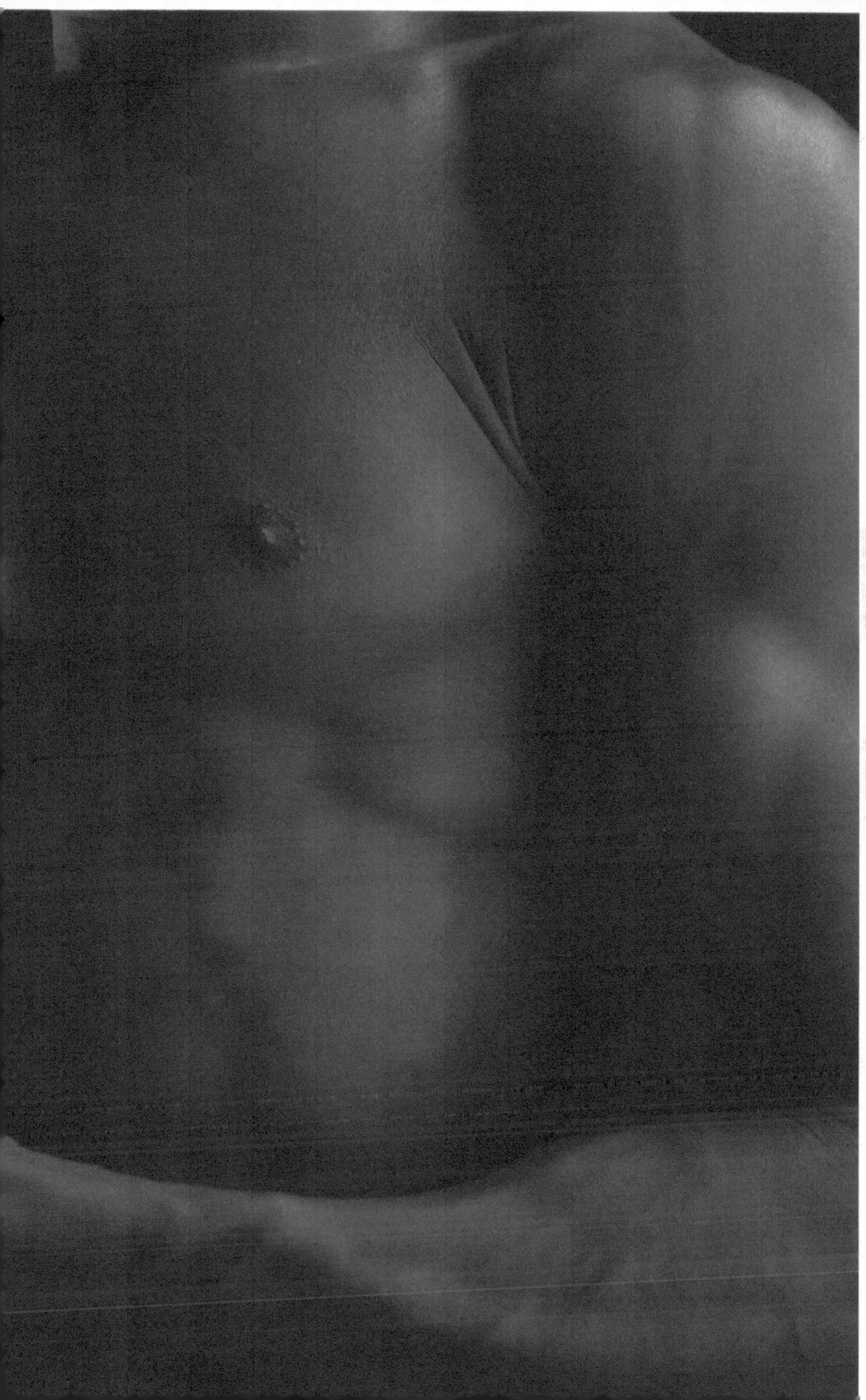

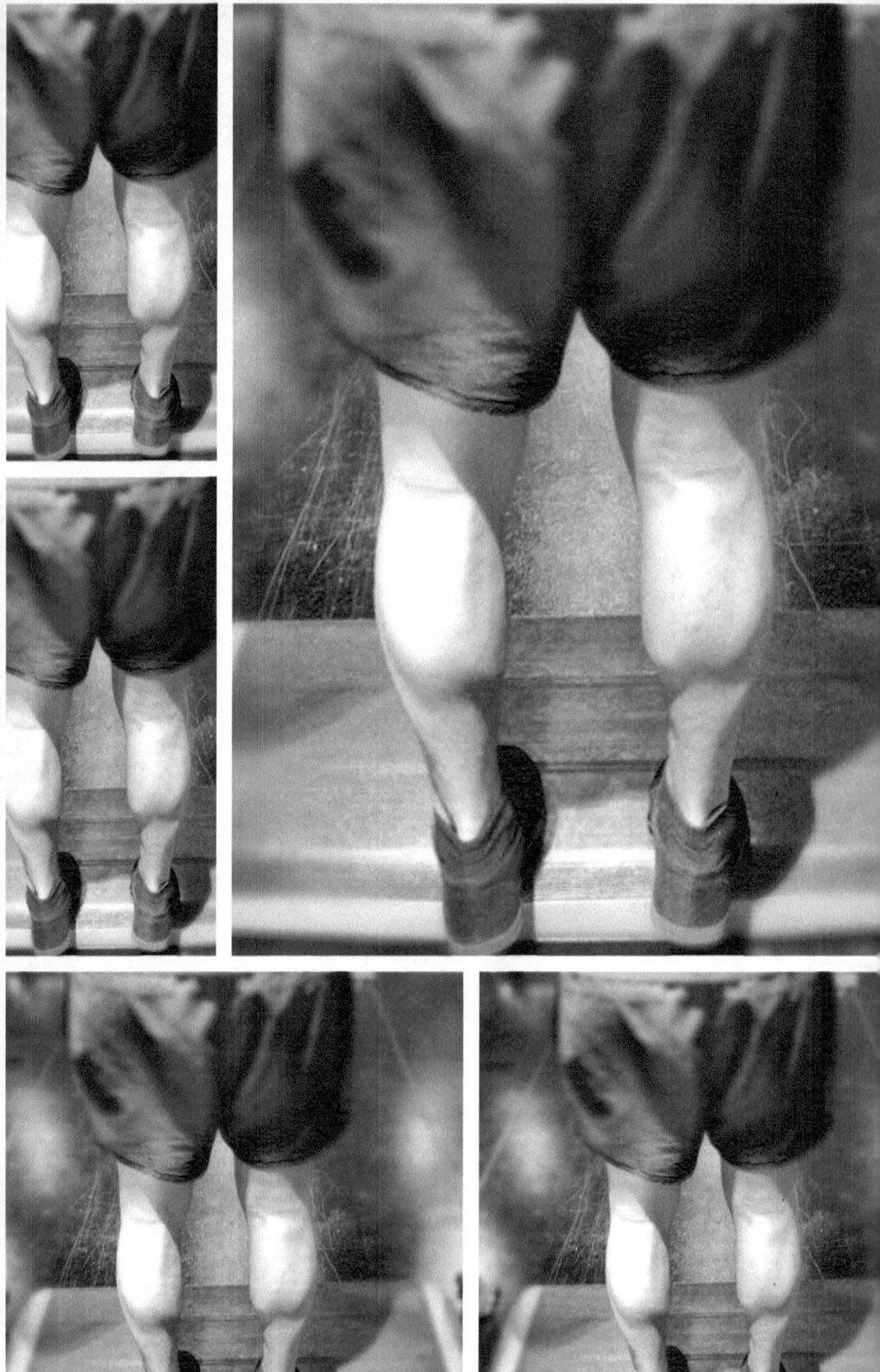

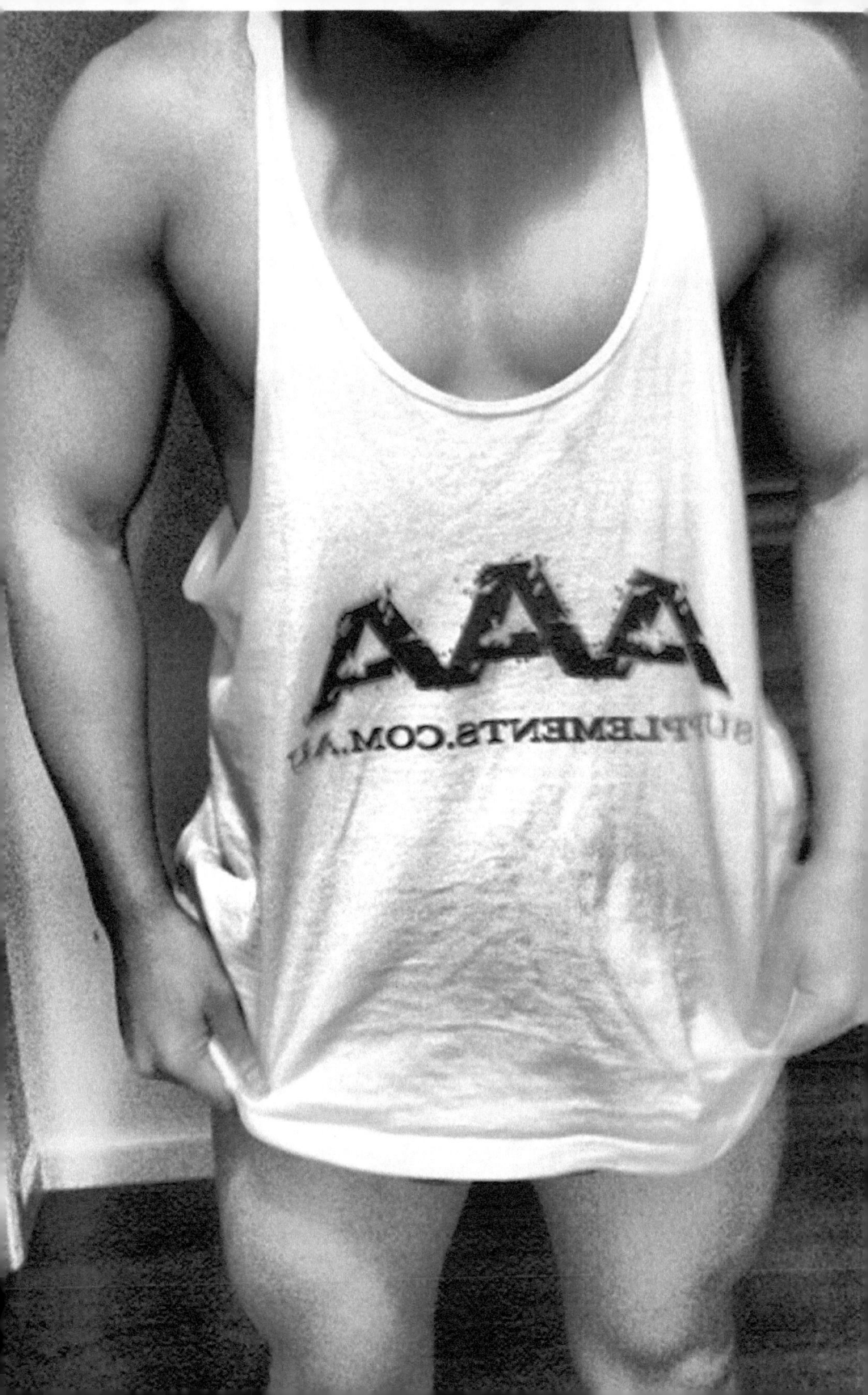

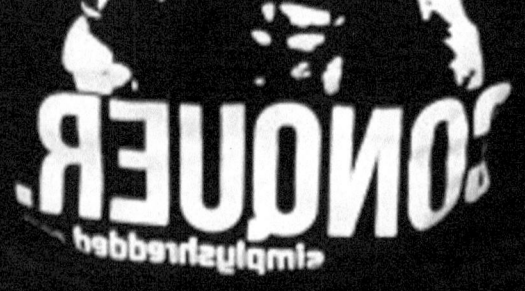

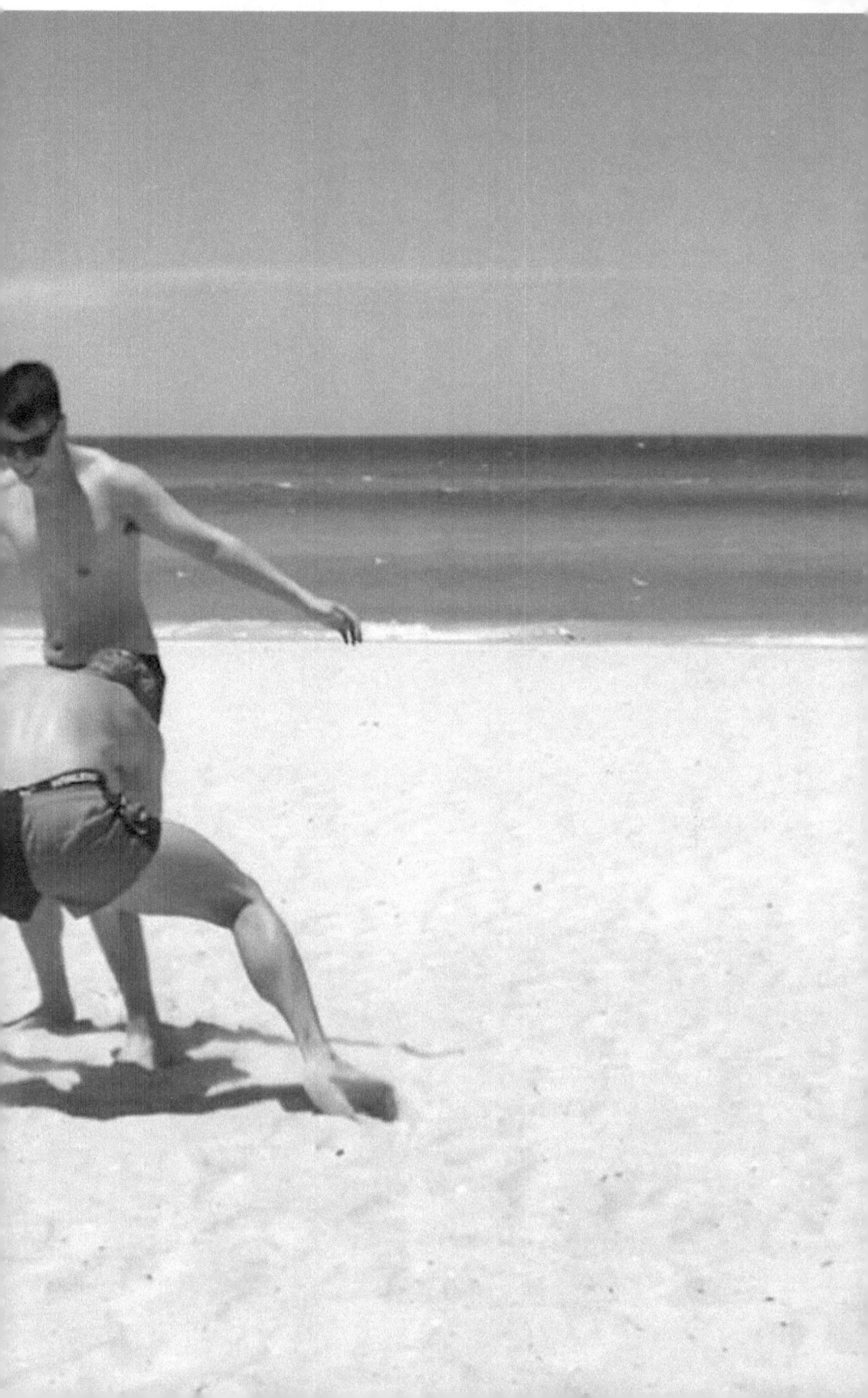

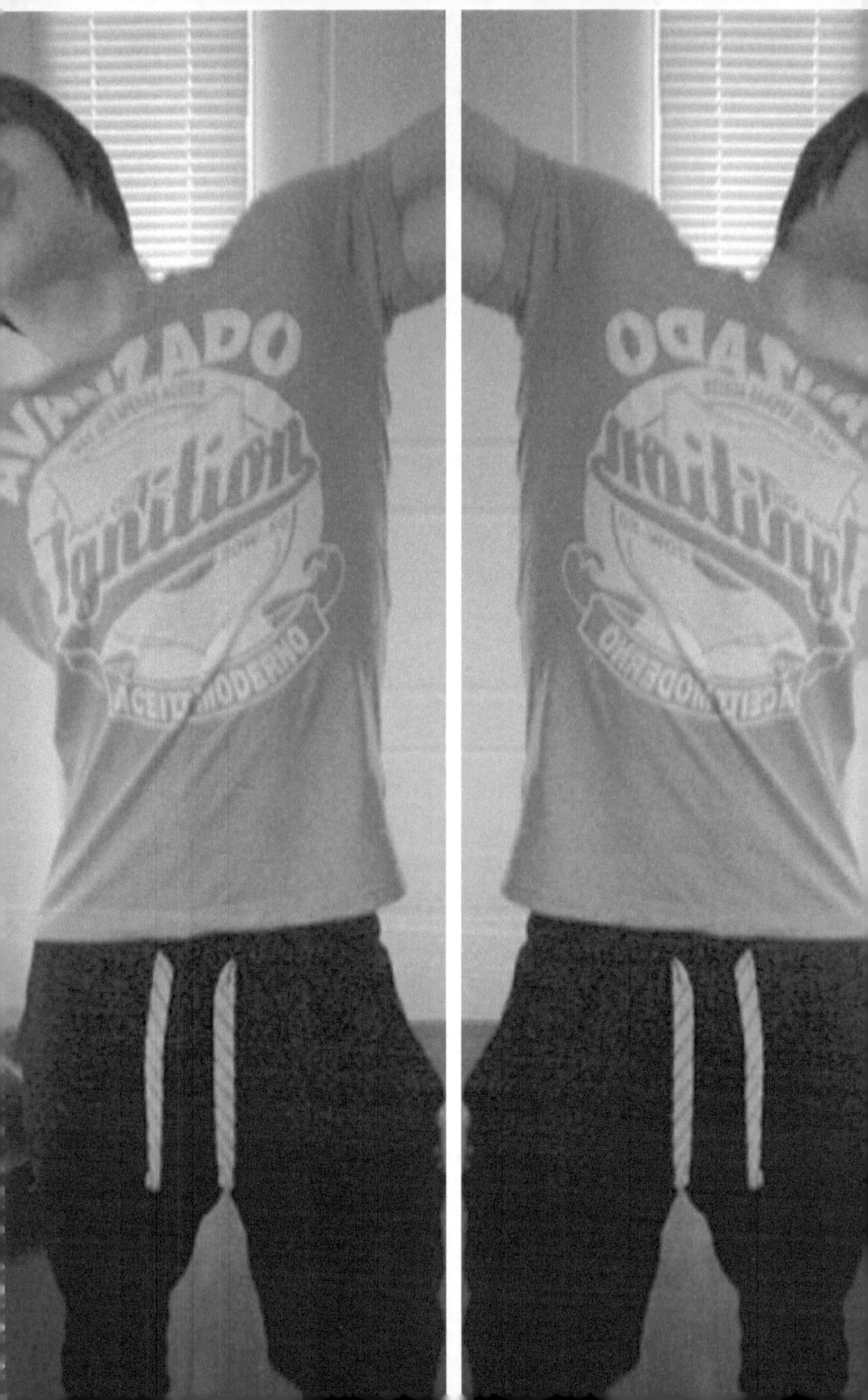

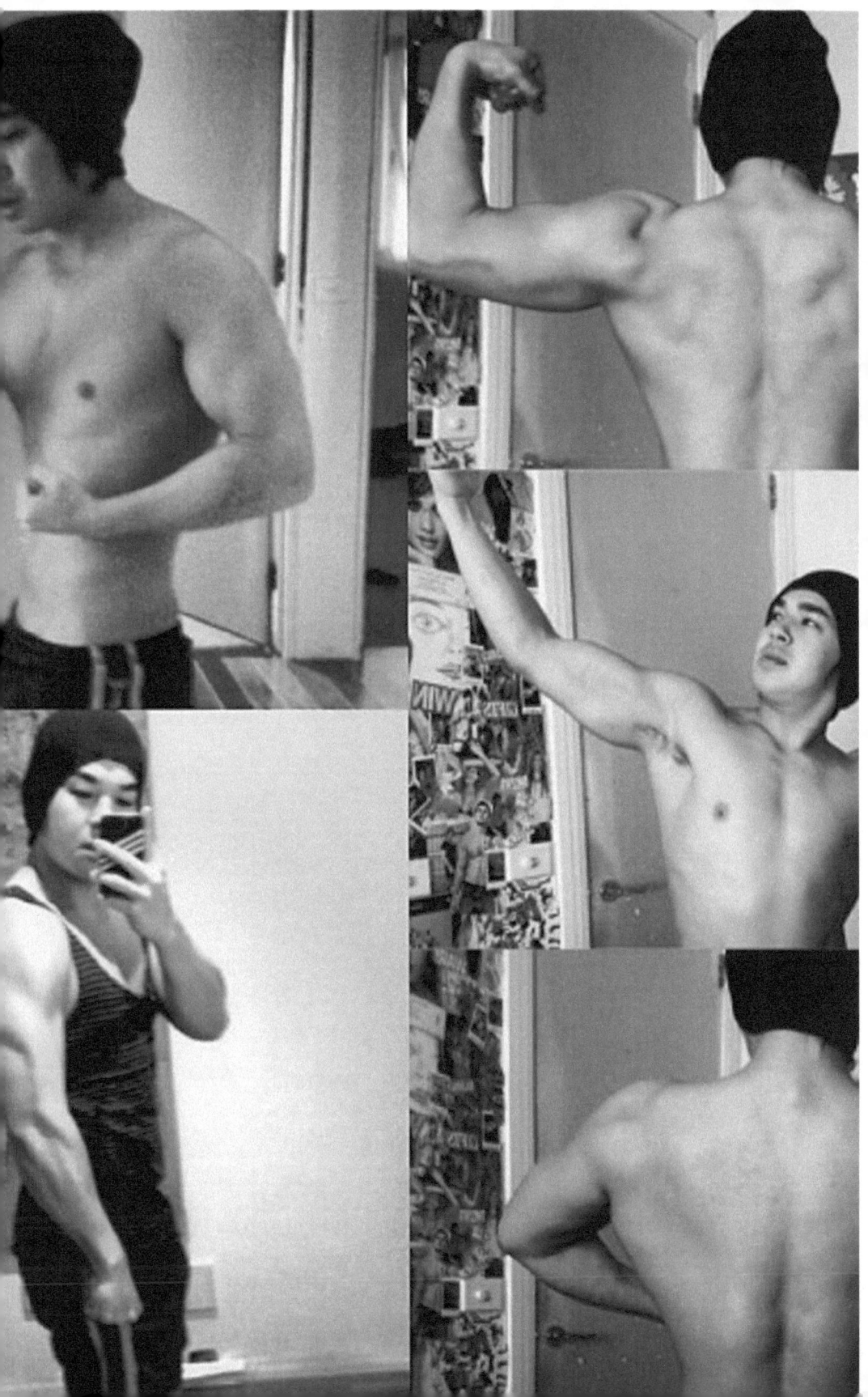

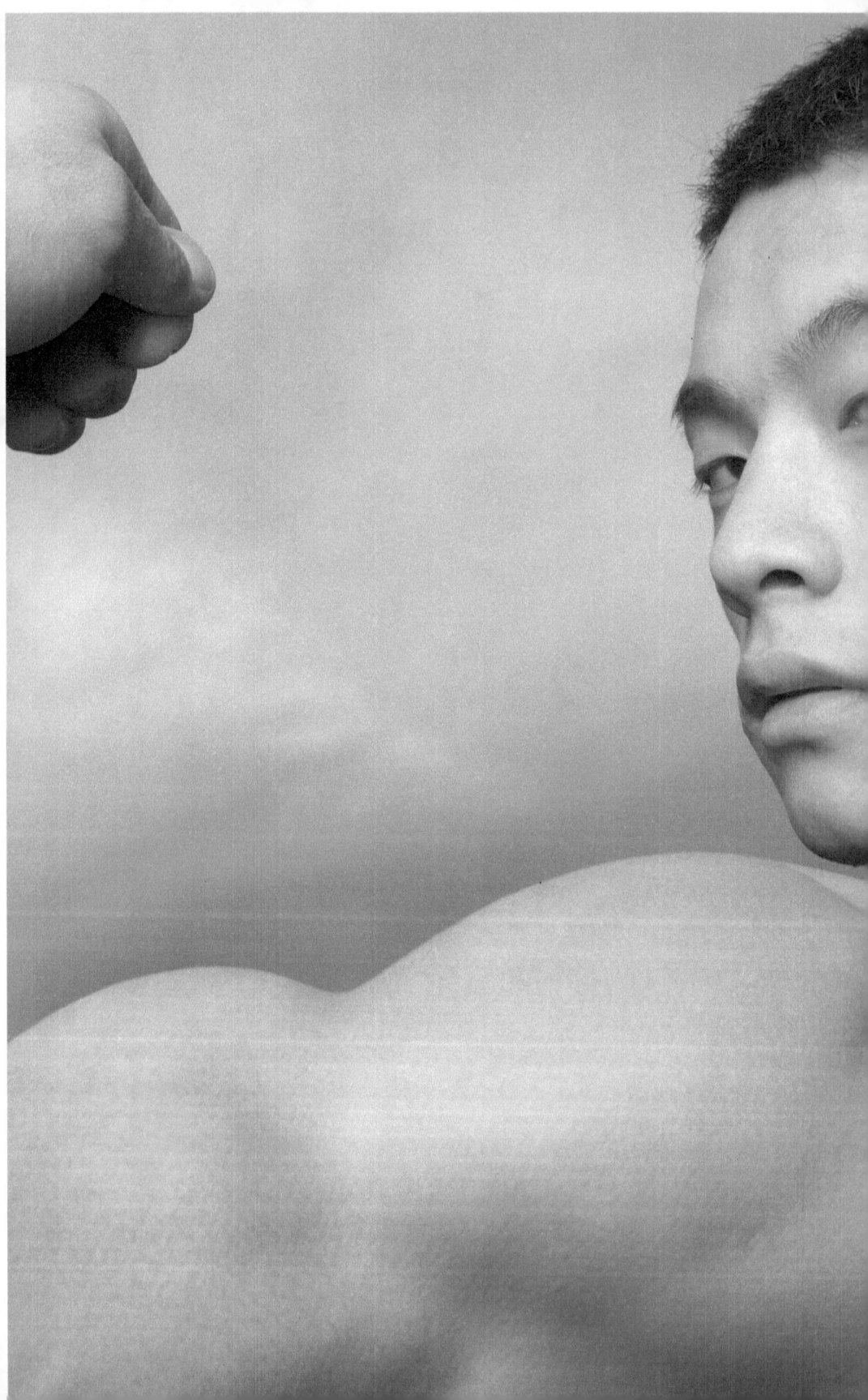

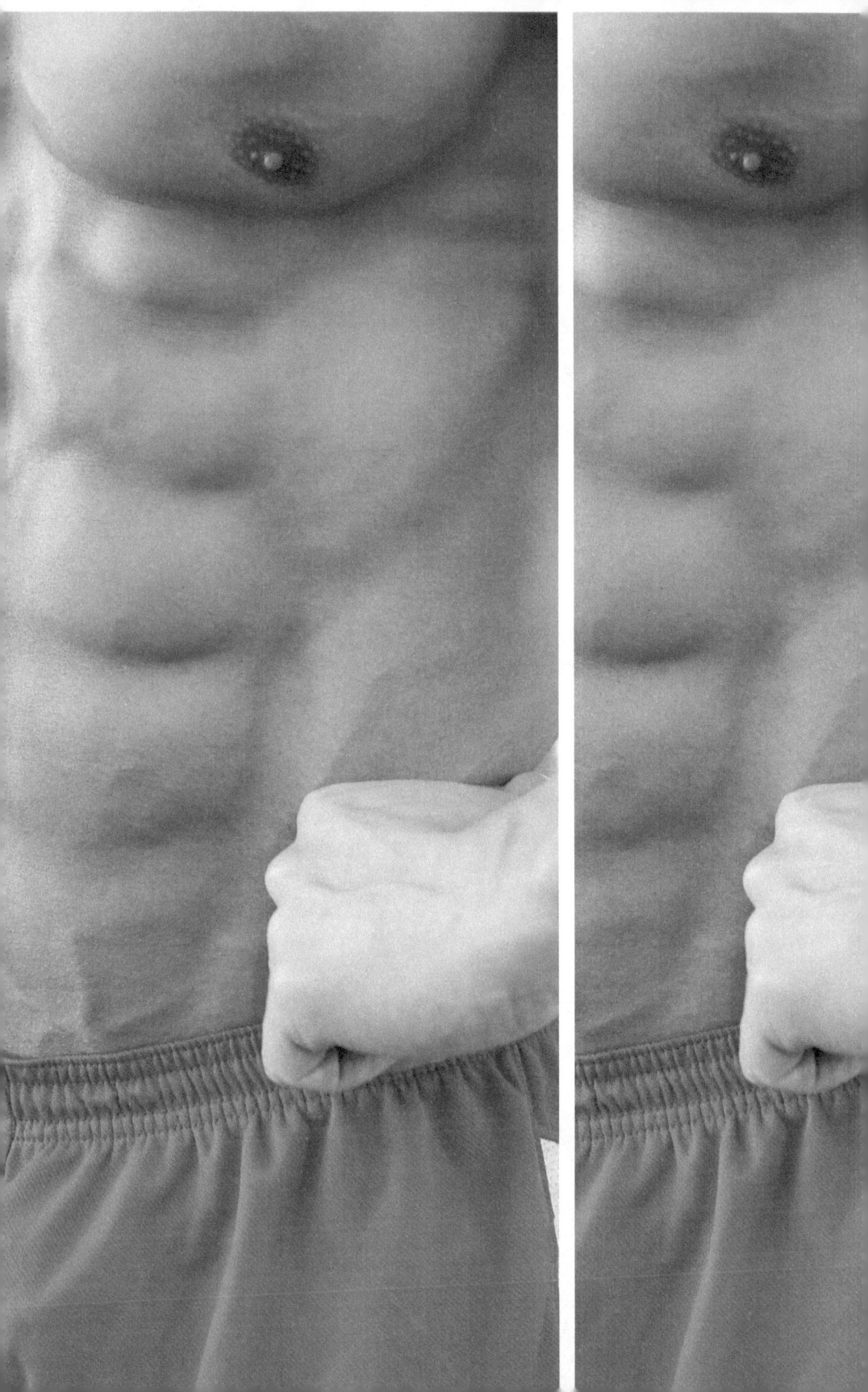

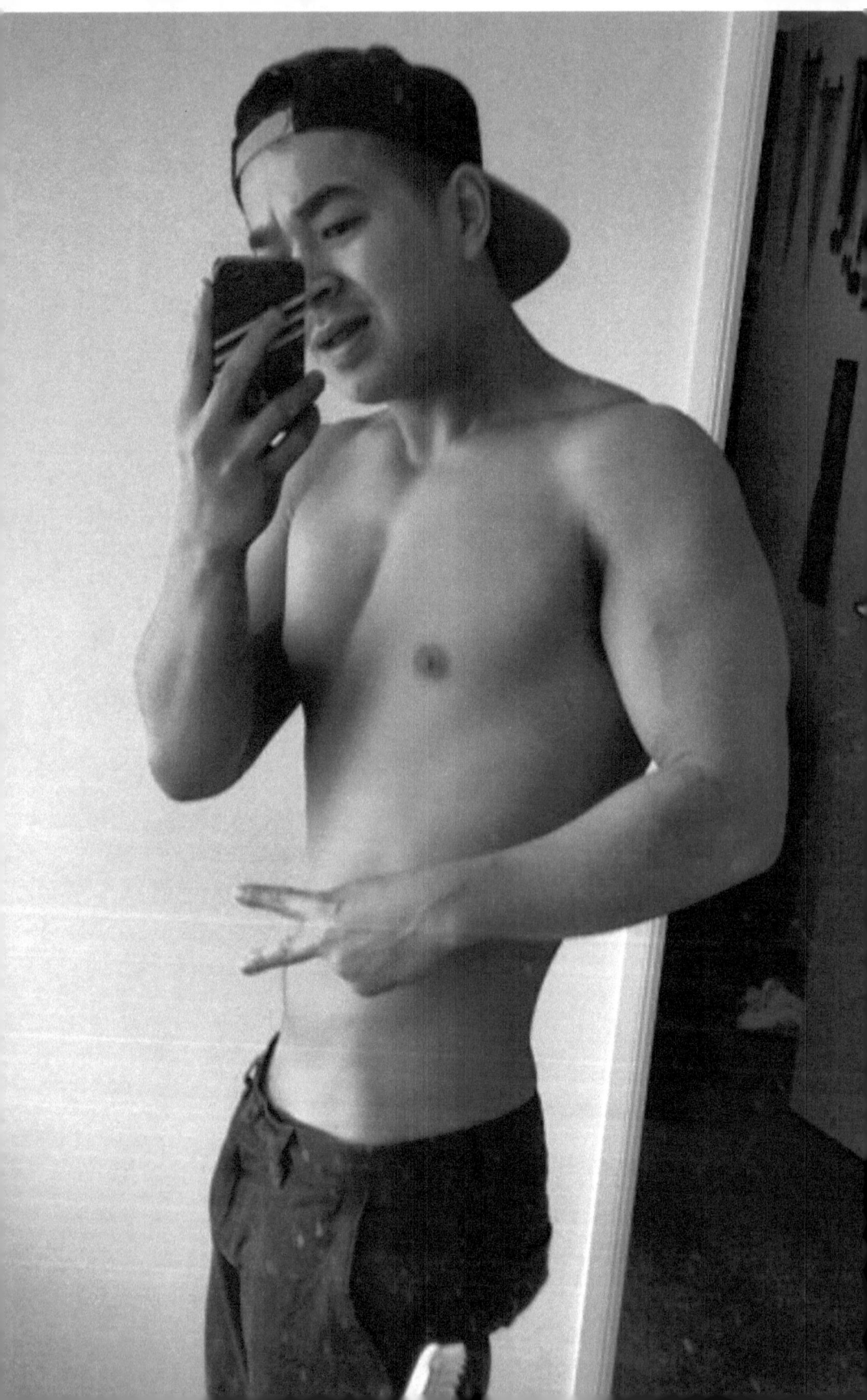

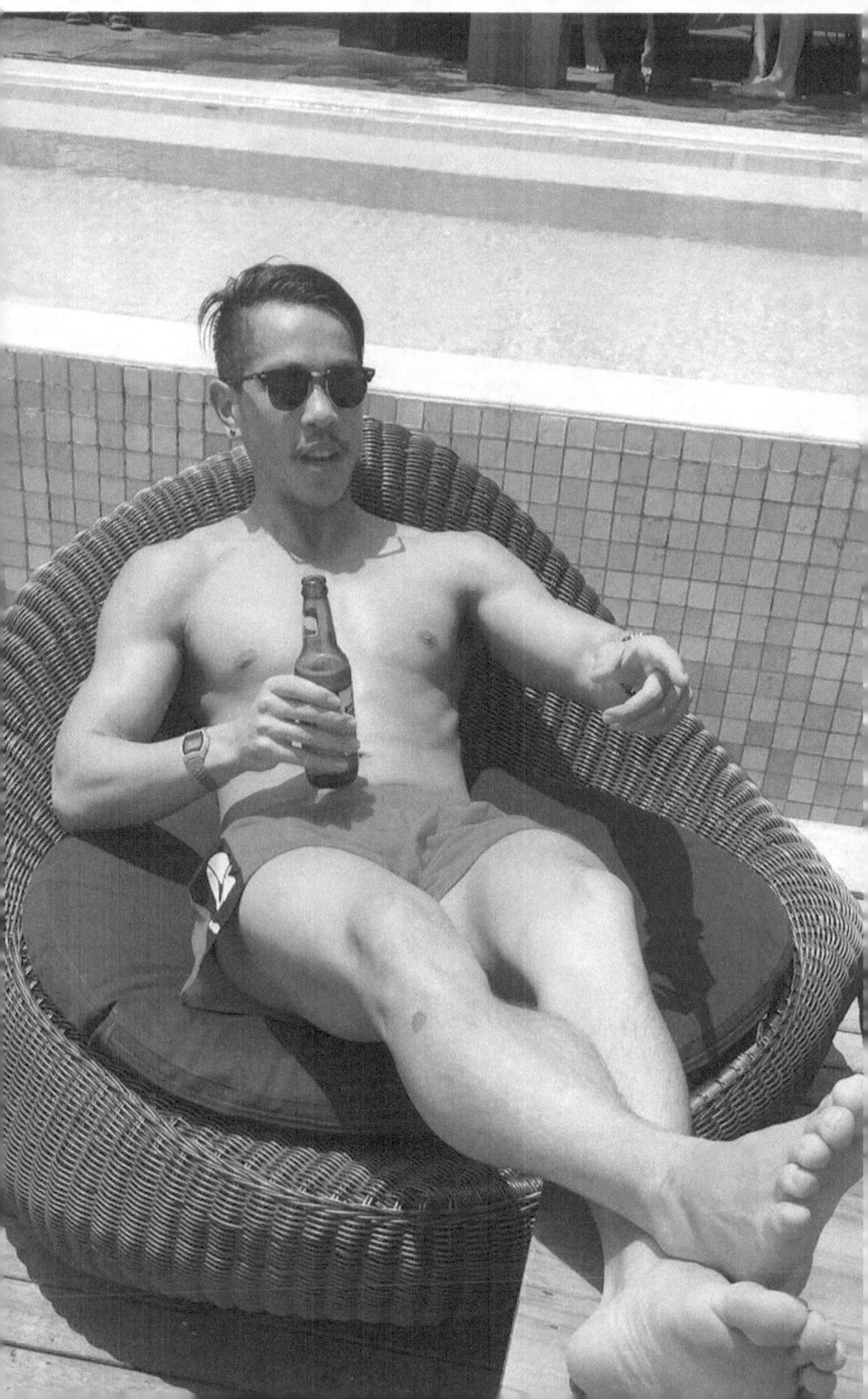

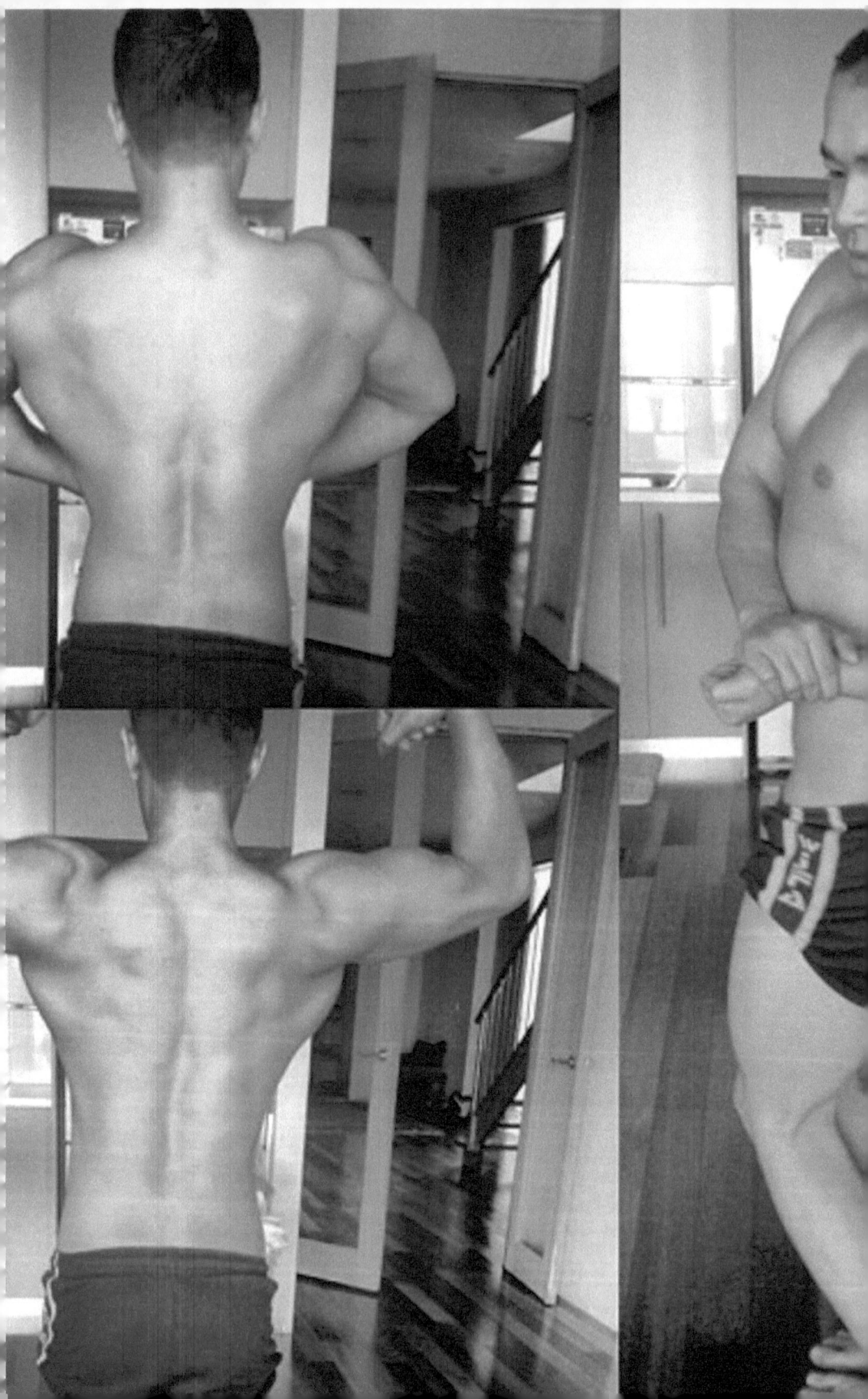

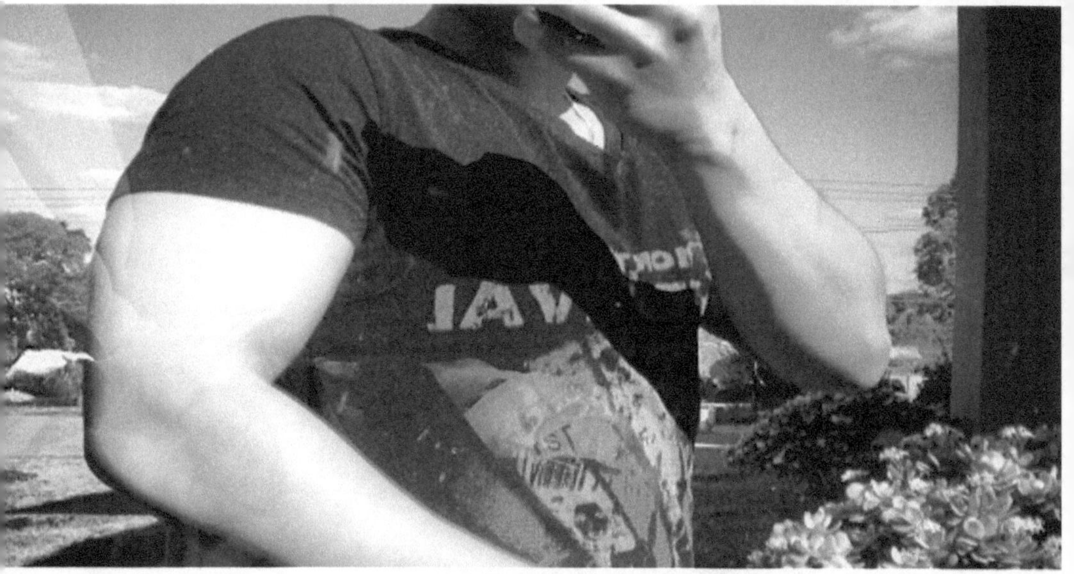

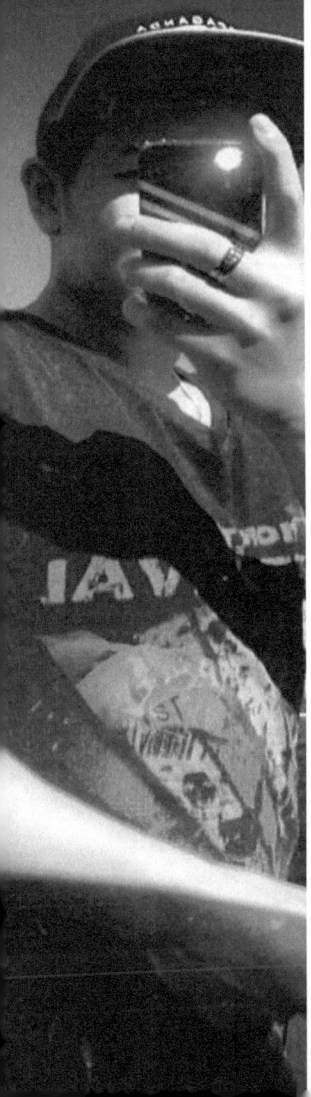

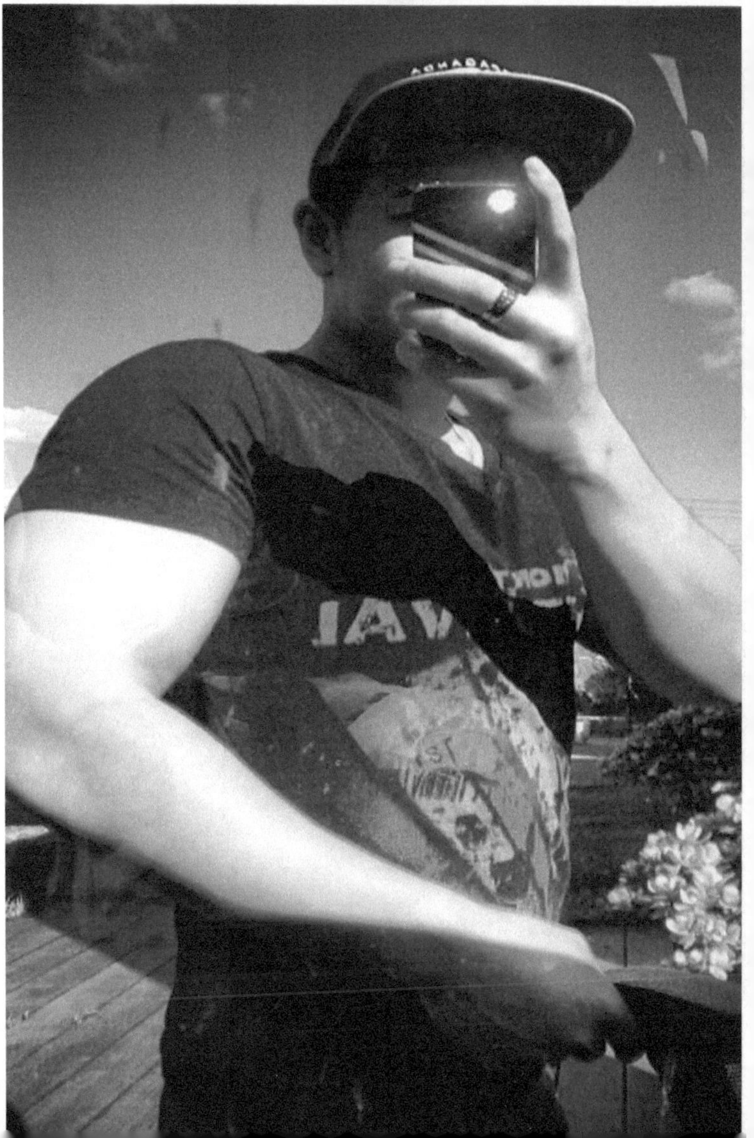

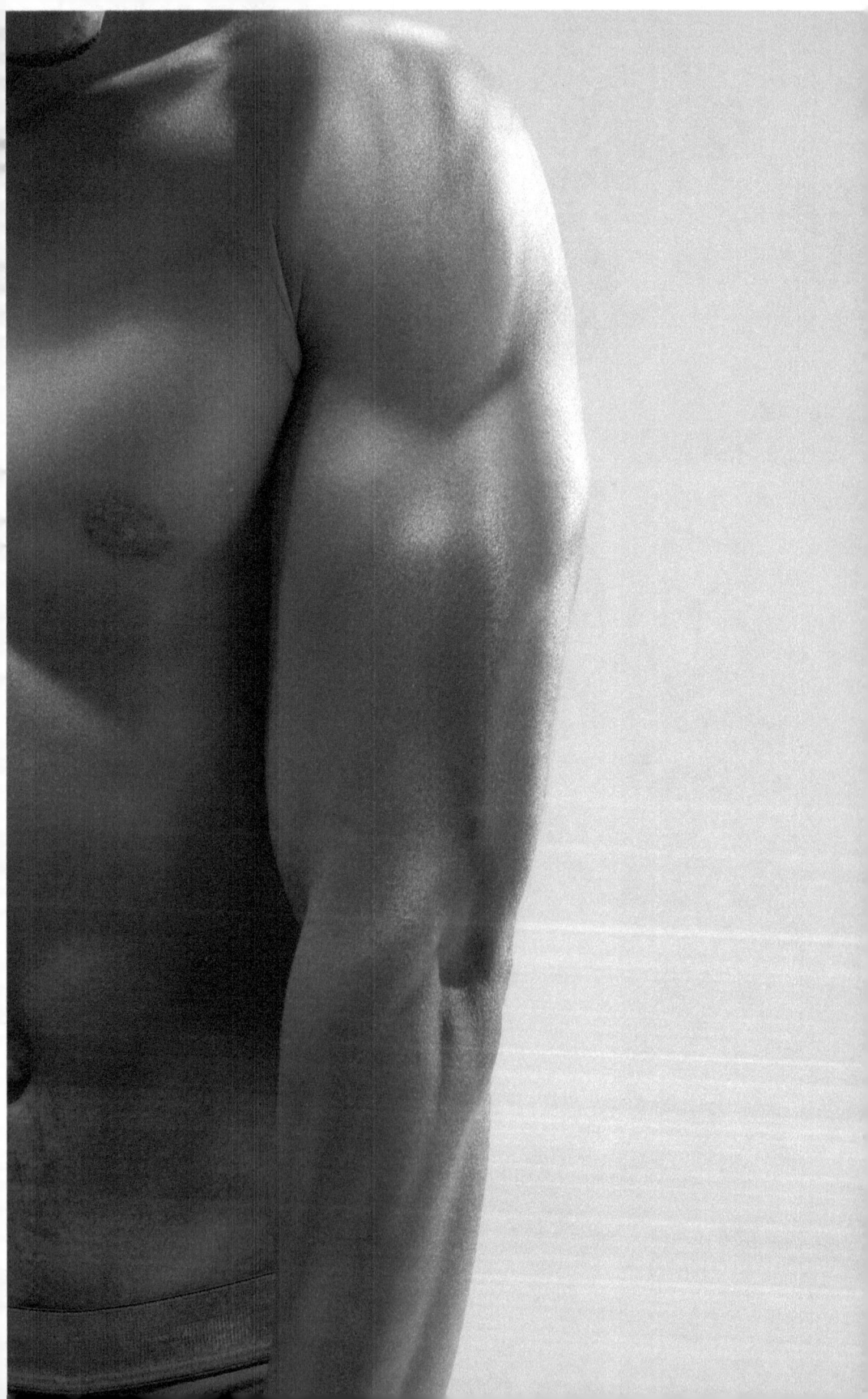

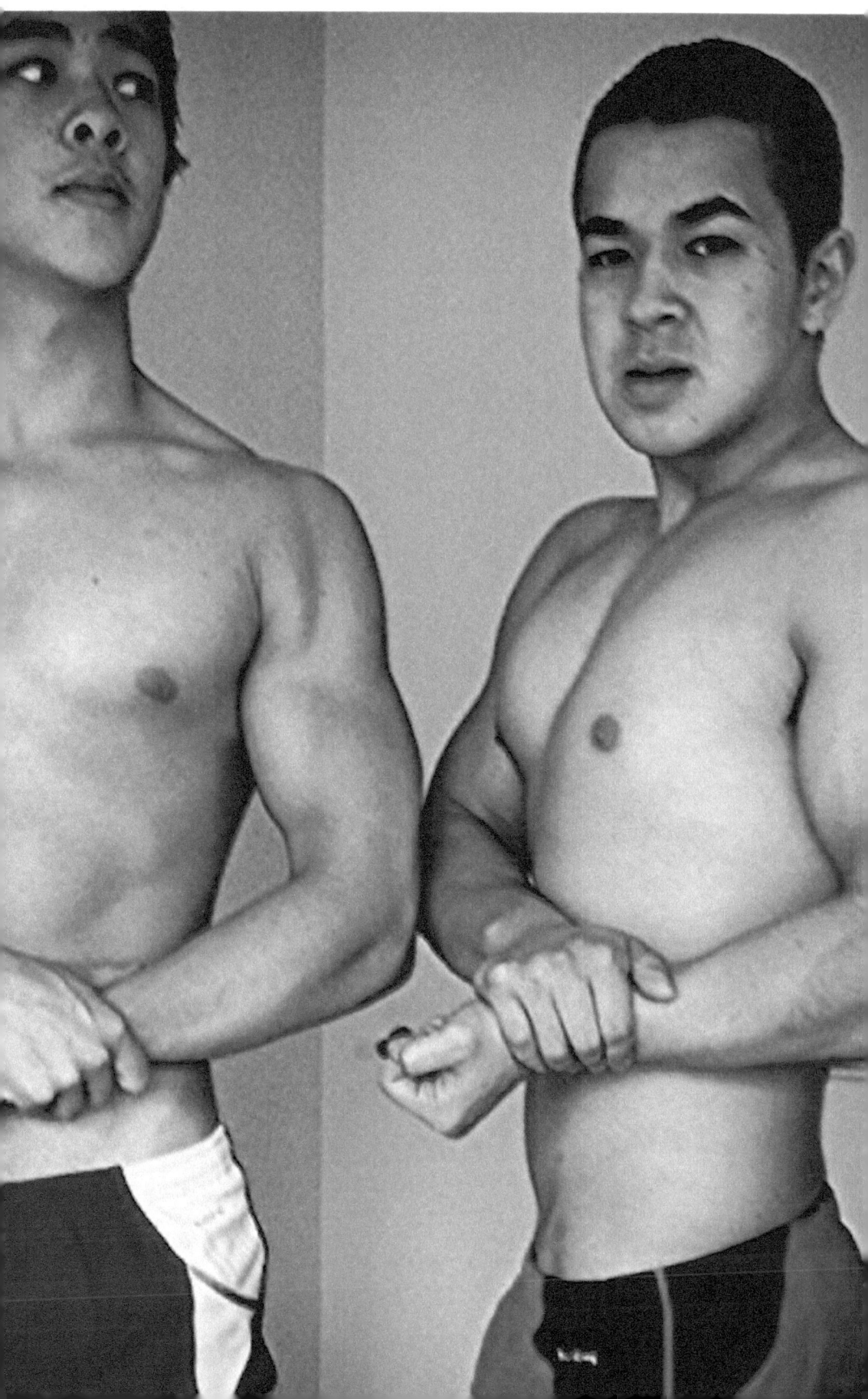

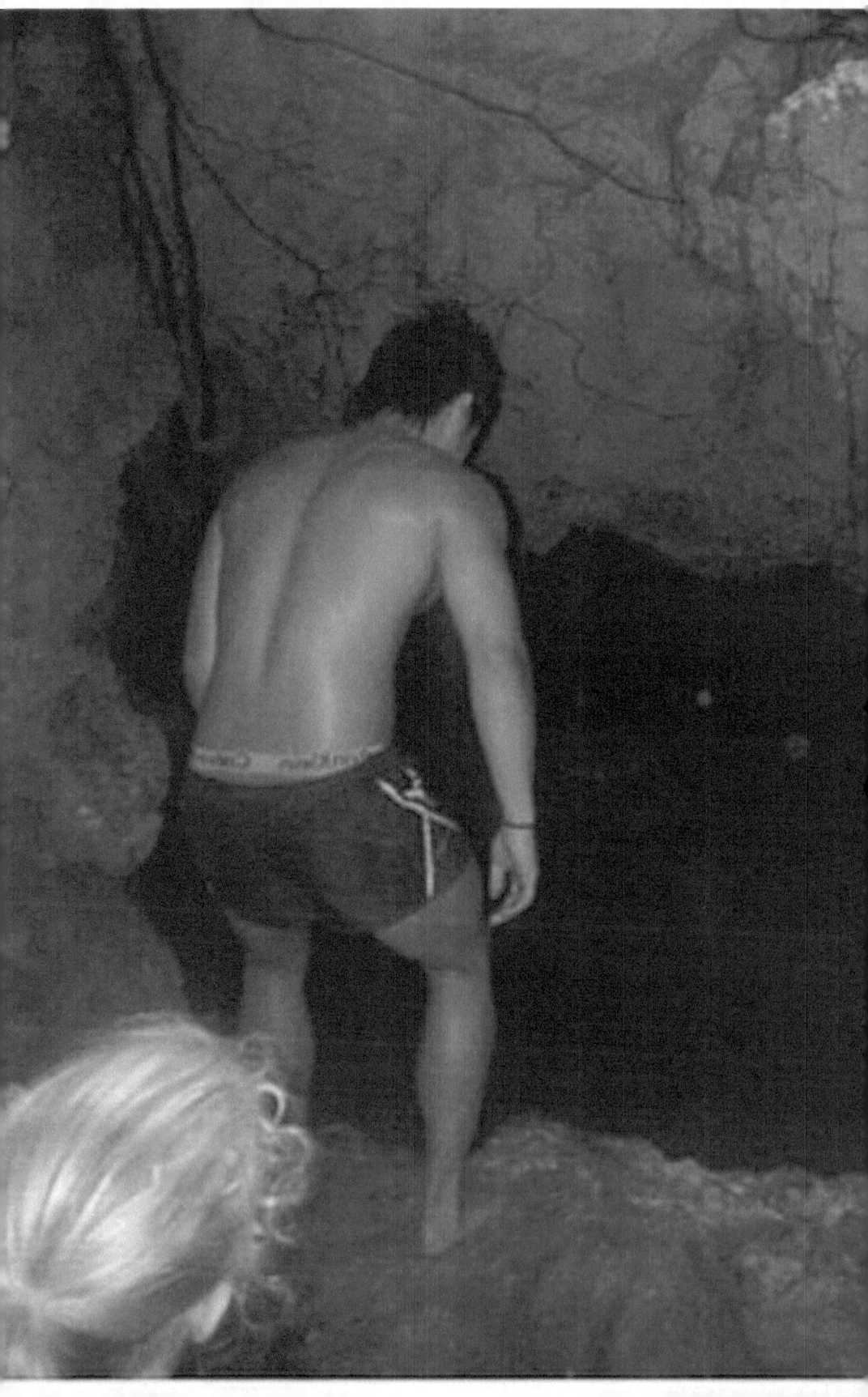

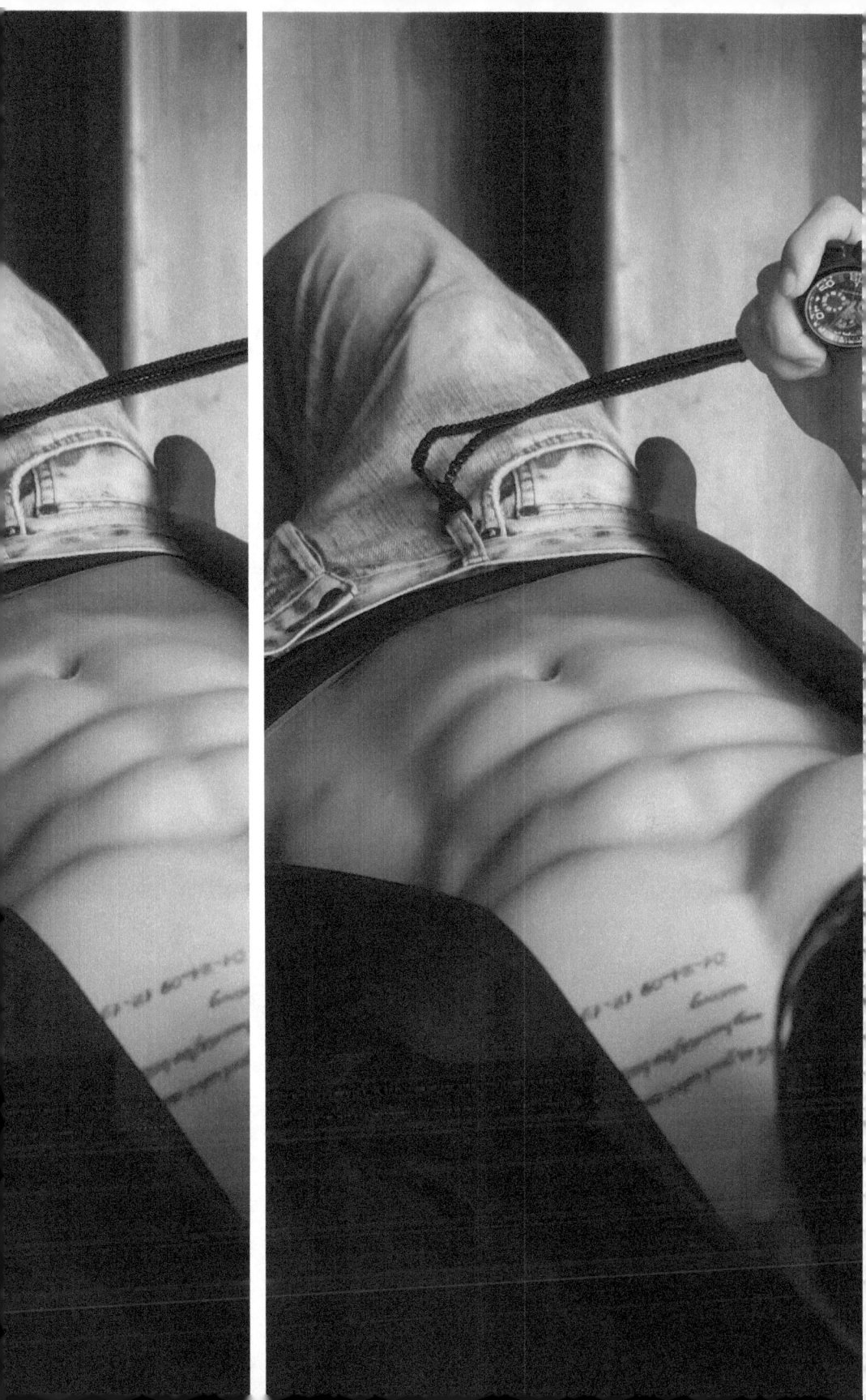

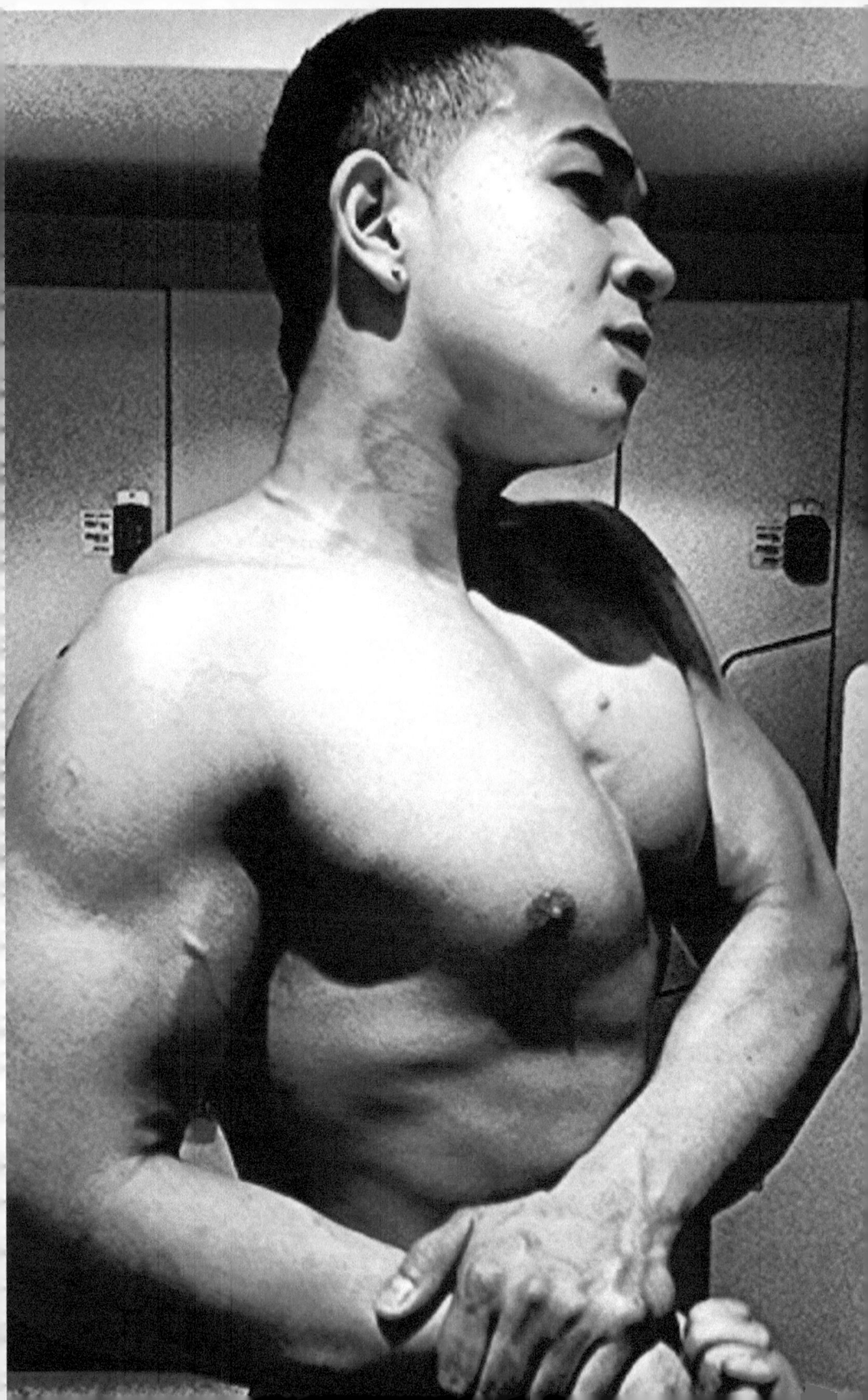

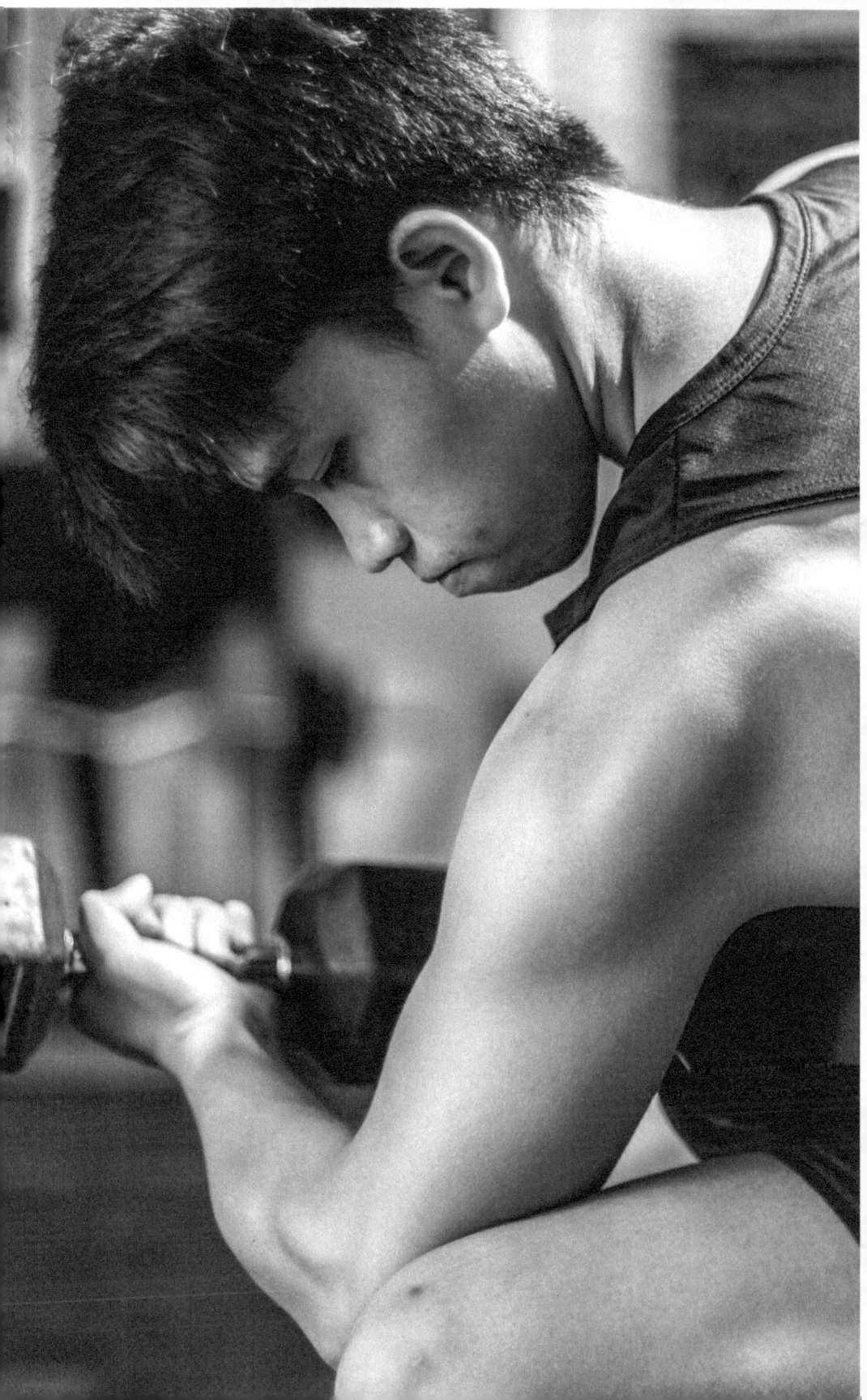

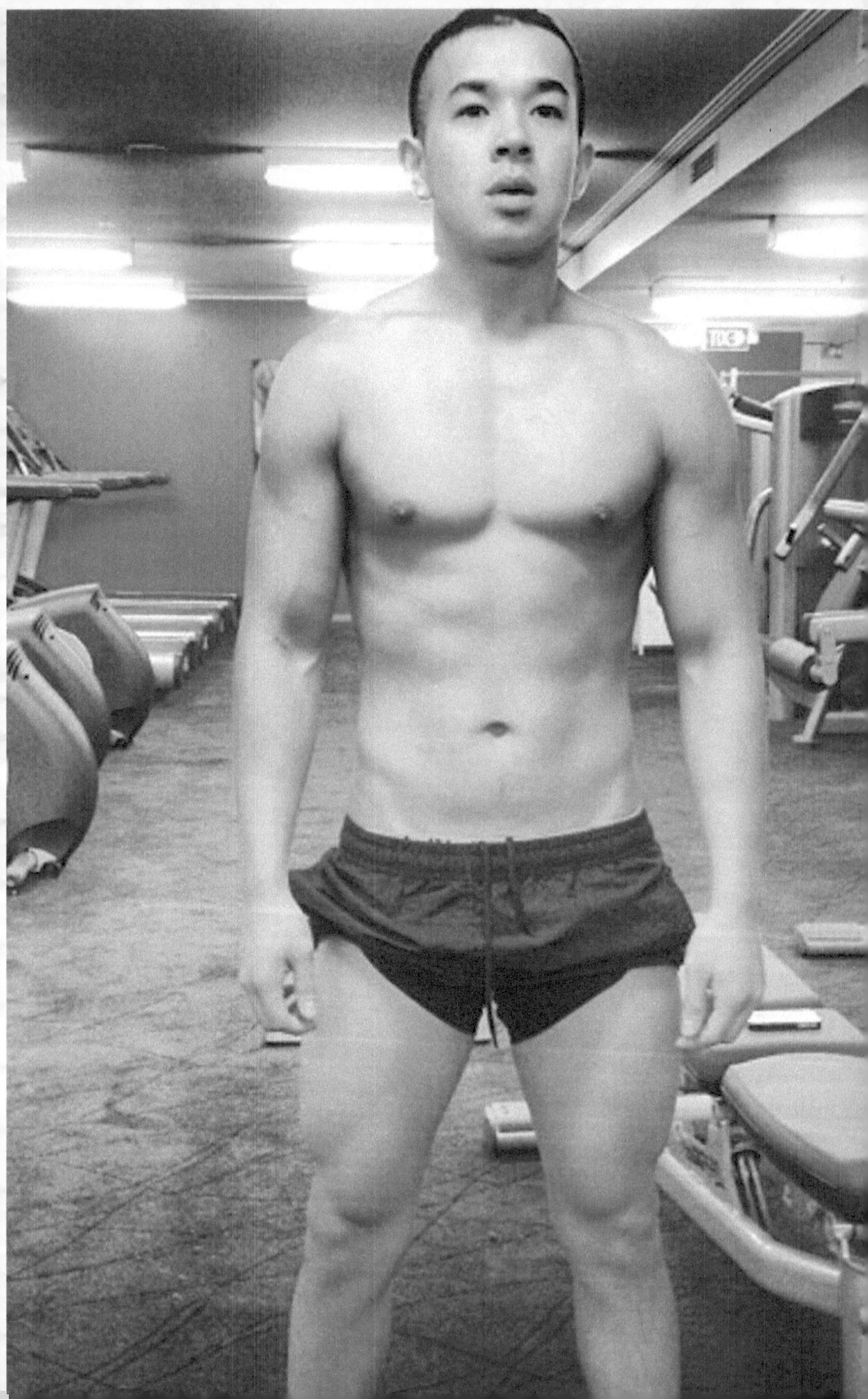

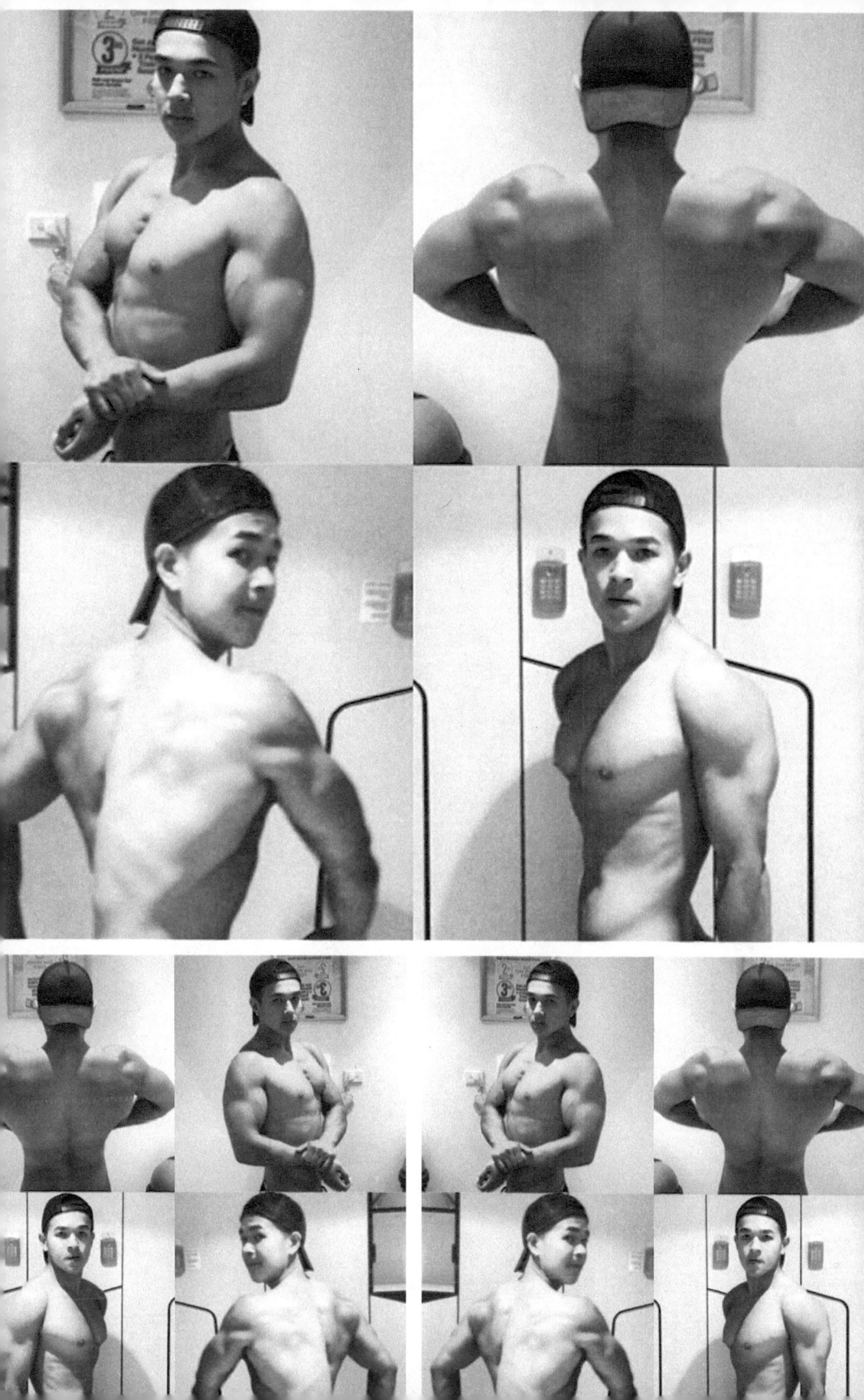

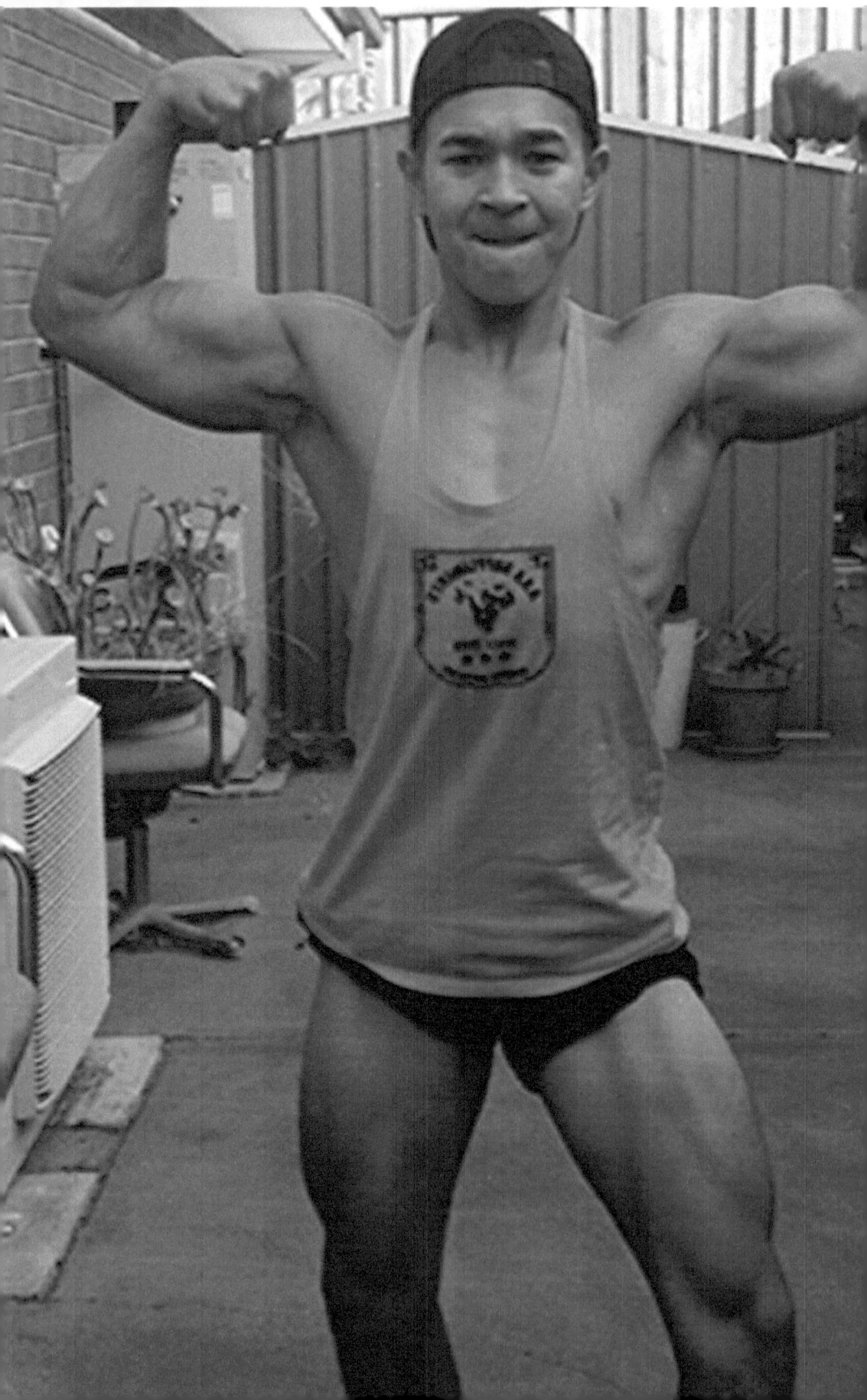

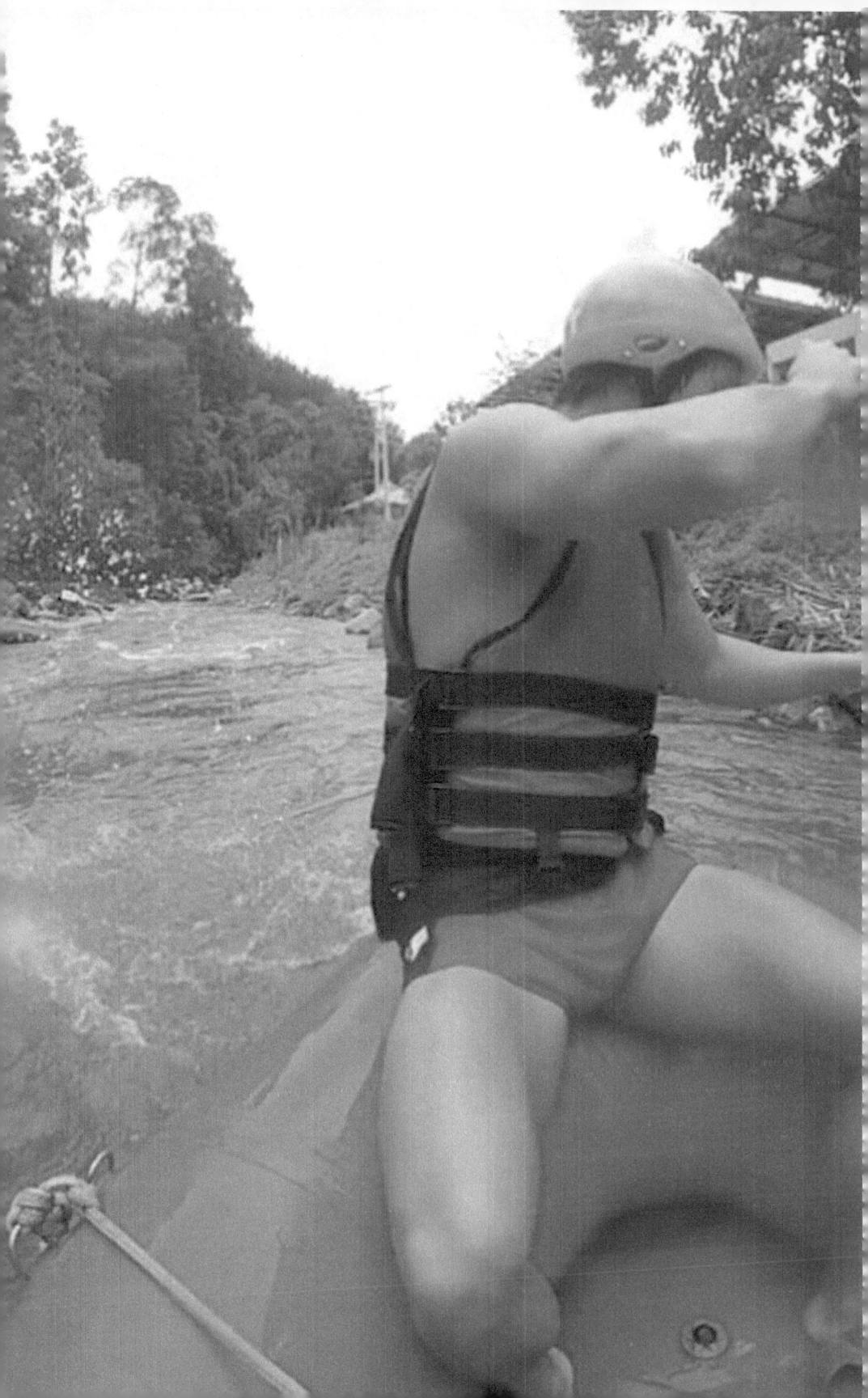

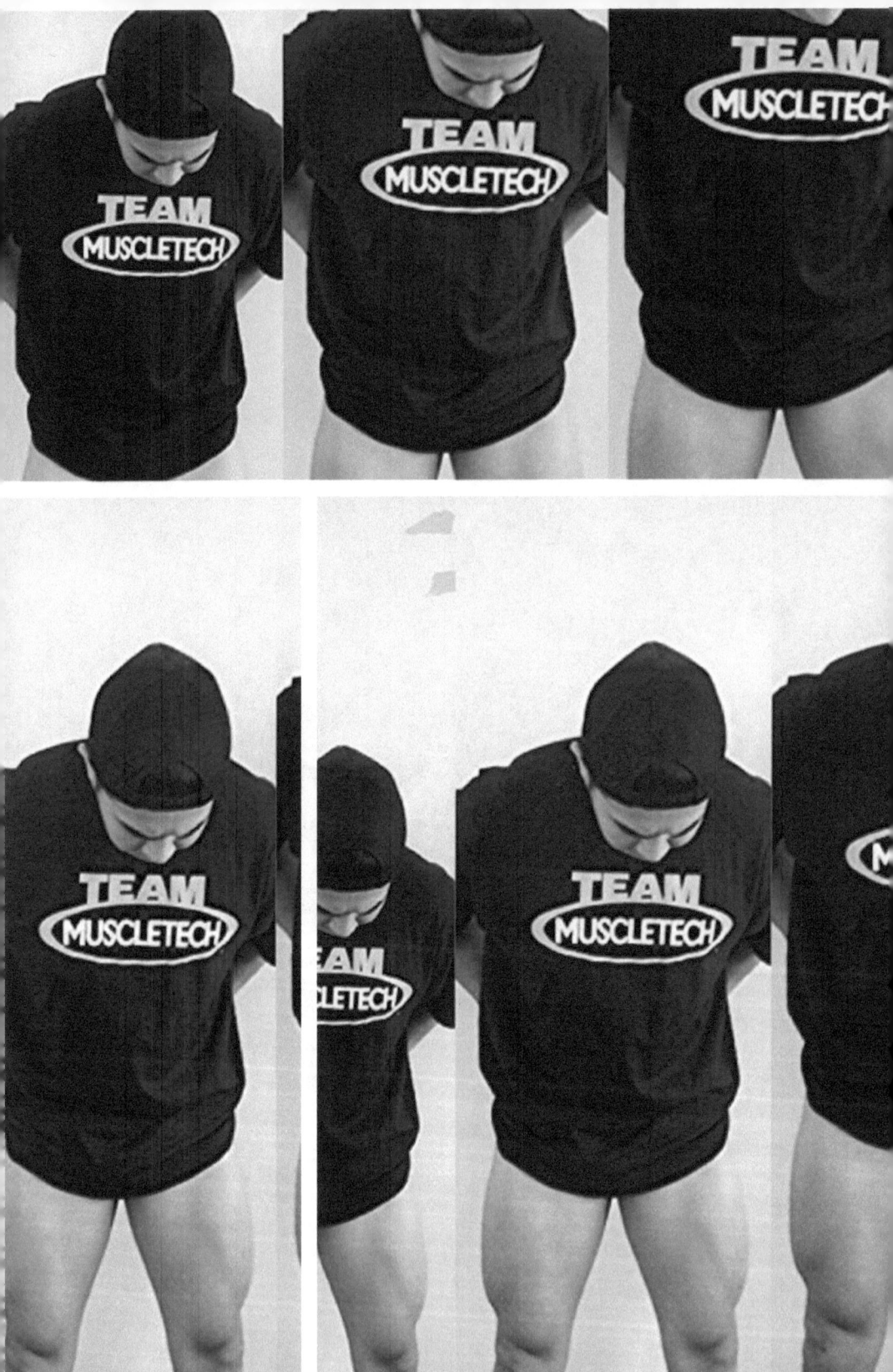

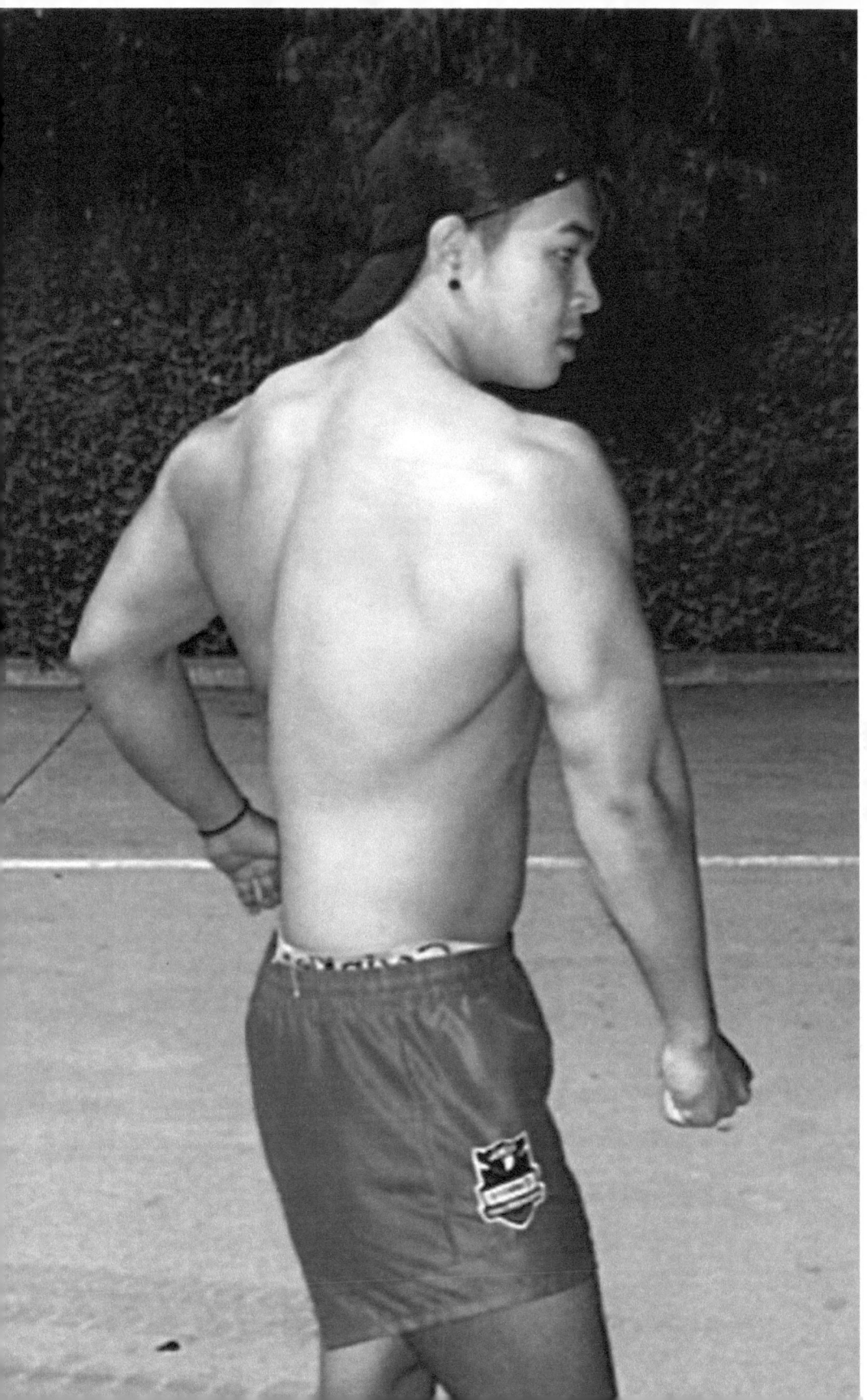

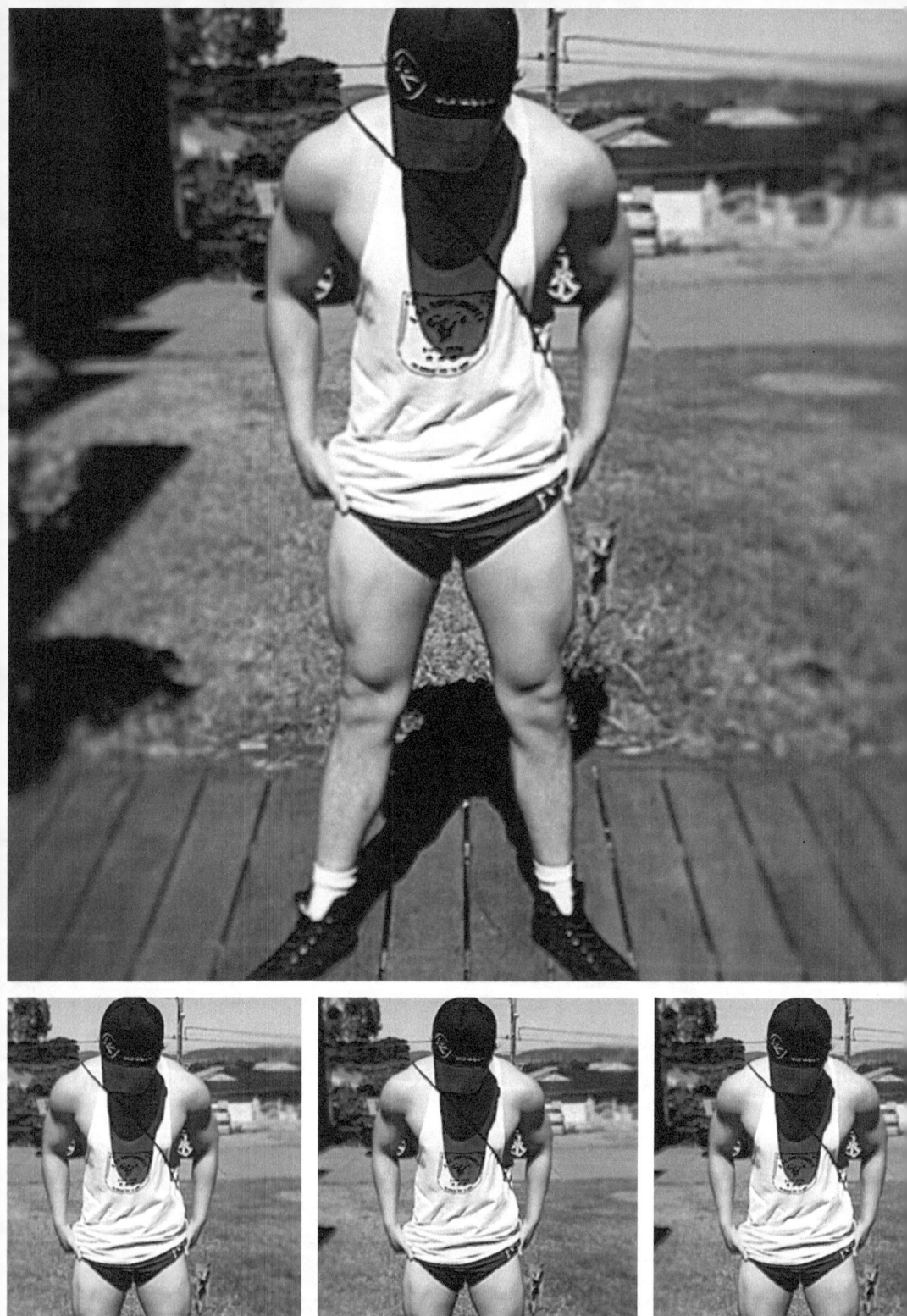

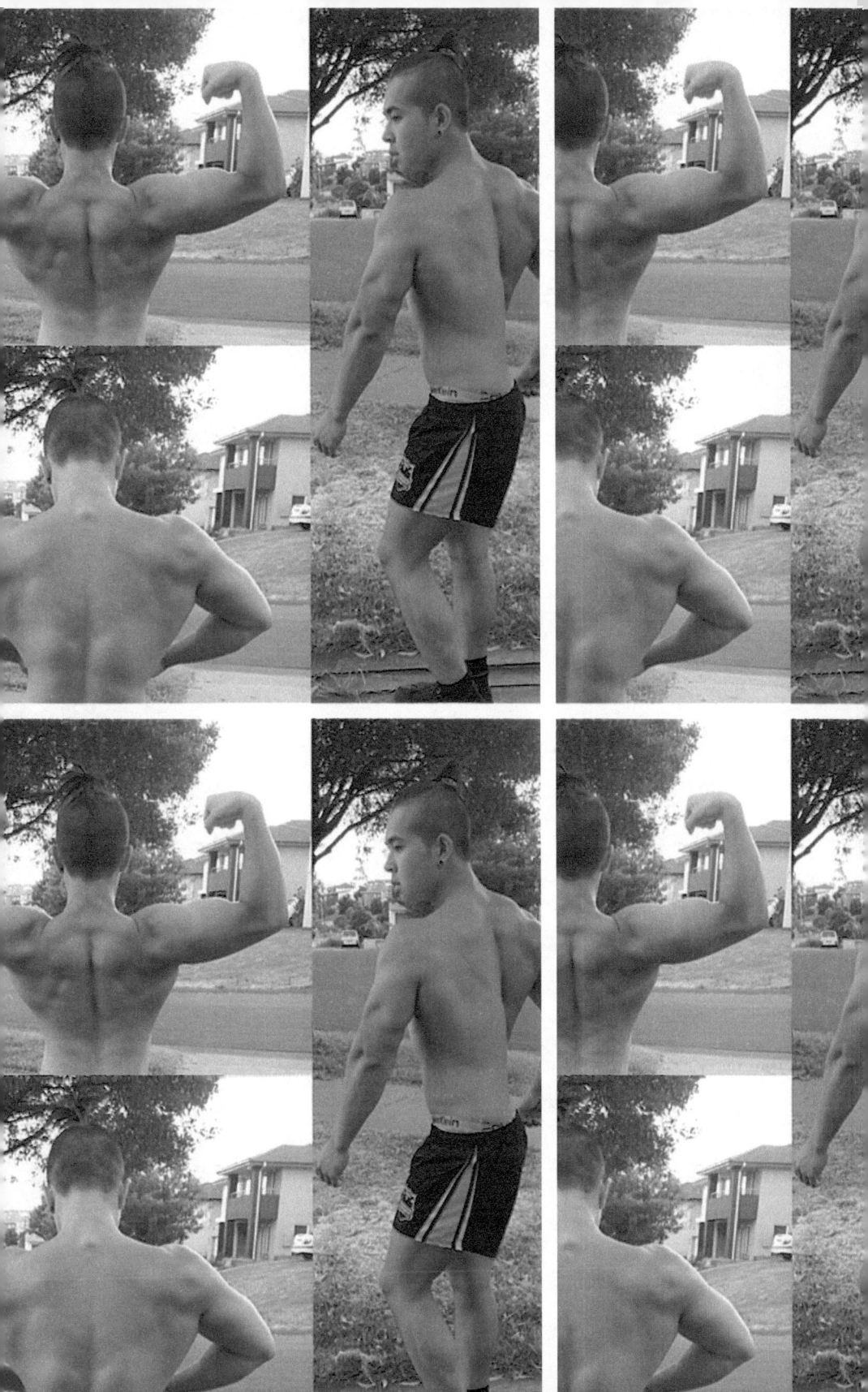

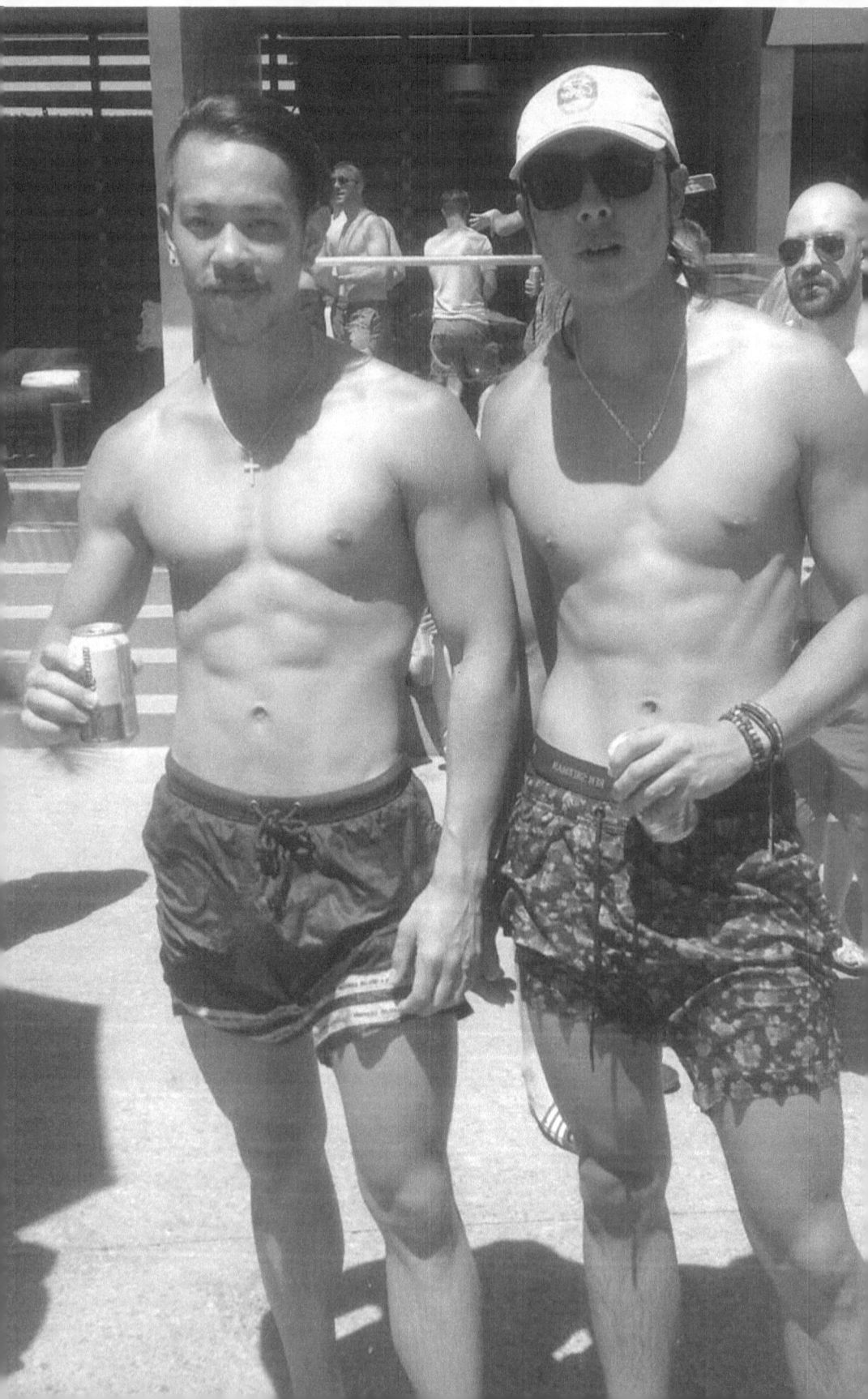

www.ingramcontent.com/pod-product-compliance
Lightning Source LLC
Chambersburg PA
CBHW021044180526
45163CB00005B/2285